KU-413-592

snowboarding
skills

snowboarding
skills

The back-to-basics essentials for all levels

Cindy Kleh

A QUINTET BOOK

Published in 2002 by Silverdale Books

An imprint of Bookmart Limited
Registered number 2372865
Trading as Bookmart Limited
Desford Road
Enderby
Leicester
LE19 4AD

Copyright 2002 Quintet Publishing

All rights reserved. No part of this publication may be reproduced, stored in a retrieval system,
or transmitted in any form or by any means, electronic, mechanical, photocopying, recording,
or otherwise without the prior written permission of the copyright owner.

ISBN 1-85605 717 8

This book was designed and produced by
Quintet Publishing Limited
6 Blundell Street
London N7 7BH

Project Editor: Debbie Foy
Designer: Rod Teasdale
Photographer: Jed Jacobson
Creative Director: Richard Dewing
Publisher: Oliver Salzmann

With thanks to Keystone (Vail Resorts), Copper Mountain, Arapahoe Basin and Winter
Park snowboarding resorts.

Manufactured in Hong Kong by Regent Publishing Services Ltd
Printed in China by Leefung-Asco Printers Limited

Grab a board and hang on!

Snowboarding is the most fun you can have with your clothes on! It's an exhilarating ride and almost anyone can learn quickly to glide downhill with confidence. Everyone's getting on board: moms, dads and kids, older folks, and even not-so-rad folks.

For a skier, it's an easy conversion. With a basic knowledge of how gravity, snow and edges work, skiers need only to apply that to a new edging sensation, rocking heel to toe instead of side to side. Snowboarding is easier on the knees than skiing and conquering powder with half the effort hooks most skiers onto the sport. Familiar trails take on a fresh, new look from a sideways perspective.

Best of all, self-expression rules! There is no right or wrong way to ride or dress, and more room to be yourself. It's not how you look, but how you feel—and snowboarding feels great.

For those new to downhill snow sports, be forewarned: riding a snowboard is extremely addictive! The first time you link a heel turn with a toe turn and back to a heel turn, you will feel the grace of riding a snowboard and something changes in you forever. You are no longer someone who has *tried* snowboarding, you *are* a snowboarder. Each session on snow will be a breakthrough, as skills that seemed so difficult and uncomfortable on your first day become more energy-efficient and automatic.

And then, the first powder day comes and your "perma-grin" lasts for weeks. Floating though deep, dry snow is pure heaven, and once bitten by the "pow bug" you will spend the rest of your life trying to recreate that wonderful feeling, even if it means calling in sick for work or forgetting to buy groceries. Life has new priorities, new challenges...and lots of new friends.

No one can read a book and then simply go out and snowboard, but there are many hints on these pages that will make the process of learning easier on your ego and your backside. That's what this book is all about—getting you off the couch and dressed for action and helping you feel confident and ready for the first lesson. It will take you through the basics, from finding the right rental equipment to linking turns, it will save you from wasting energy and maybe spare you a few bruises along the way. It will even show you how to maintain your body for better performance on the slopes.

Who knows where a snowboard could take you? Through quiet, untracked powder in the trees...to the top of a podium surrounded by cheering crowds... or free-floating through big air caught off the biggest jump in the terrain park. So hop on board and get ready to experience the ride of your life!

Board Talk

180, 360 – amount of degrees of rotation in an aerial spinning maneuver

air – anytime the rider leaves the snow while attached to the snowboard

air to fakie – a trick in the *halfpipe*, where the rider approaches the wall forward, no rotation is made and the rider descends the wall riding *fakie*

angulation – using the body to increase balance and save energy while carving by bending the knees, ankles and hips to bring the body closer to the board

backside – the *heel edge* of the board; an aerial maneuver initiated from the *heel edge*

backside wall – the side of the *halfpipe* where a rider's back is to the wall; the left wall for *regulars* and right wall for *goofies*

backcountry – out-of-bounds, unpatrolled areas

bank turn – a turn made off the side of a bump or wall

bindings – adjustable devices that keep your feet attached to the snowboard

blind landing – when the rider cannot see the landing from the starting point

blindside – the *backside* or *heel side*, or to rotate (spin) toward that side, looking over the shoulder

bone – to stylize a trick by stretching out the legs to maximum degree

bonk/jib – to intentionally scrape, slide over or hit objects other than snow, such as picnic benches, logs, trail signs

bumps – A trail that is not groomed and develops troughs and *moguls* from frequent skier/rider use

butt-check – to touch down on your buttocks on a *heelside turn* or jump, but recover to your feet

carving – a turn that leaves a clean rut in the snow with no *skidding*

center of gravity – just inside your navel

corduroy – freshly groomed snow

drop in – enter the *halfpipe*

duckfoot – stance with both feet pointing away from each other

edge angle – the angle between the base of a snowboard and the slope

edging – using the edge of the snowboard against the slope and against gravity to control speed

effective edge – the length of the snowboard edge that touches the snow when turning

fakie – riding a board opposite to your normal stance, i.e. backward or *switch* stance

falling leaf sideslip – *traversing* the slope on only one edge

fall line – the path that a ball would fall if left on a slope

flats – portions of the mountain where there is no incline

forward lean – the degree to which a boot or binding forces your shins, calves and knees forward

freerider – a rider that uses the whole mountain and borrows from all disciplines of snowboarding

freestyle rider – a rider that specializes in *air*, spins, riding *fakie*, and *halfpipe*

front foot – the foot attached closest to the *nose* of the board; for *goofy* stance, the right foot; for *regular* stance, the left foot

frontside – *toeside* of the board; an aerial maneuver initiated from the *toeside* edge

frontside wall – when looking down the *pipe*, the right wall for *regular*-footers, the left wall for *goofies*

garland – a series of incomplete turns on one edge that leave a track in the snow resembling a Christmas tree garland

goofy – stance where the right foot is in front and the left foot is in back (see *regular*)

green slope – a beginner trail; easiest terrain

halfpipe – a feature dug out of the side of a hill that resembles a huge pipe cut in half. The halfpipe's vertical walls are used to launch aerial maneuvers

hard boots – plastic snowboard boots that resemble ski boots and attach to the board with *plate bindings*

hardpack – icy snow conditions

heel edge – the edge of the snowboard closest to the rider's heels

heel drag/toe drag – when the rider's feet are longer than the board is wide and hang over the edge of the board, causing friction with the slope and *sketching* out on turns

heelside turns – turns that begin on the *toe edge* and finish on the *heel edge*

highback – the hard plastic piece of a *strap binding* that comes up from the heel area and allows a rider with *soft boots* to lean back and gain leverage on *heelside* turns

hip pads – pull-on stretchy shorts that are lined with padding and worn under snowboard pants, to cushion falls

hit – any jump

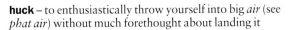

huck – to enthusiastically throw yourself into big *air* (see *phat air*) without much forethought about landing it

inchworming – a method of climbing a slope with both feet attached to the board to reposition a rider a short distance uphill

inserts – threaded metal holes on the top of the snowboard, used to mount the bindings with screws

kickers – jumps that send a rider flying high in the air

launch – to spring into huge air (see *phat air*)

leash – a safety retention device that attaches the front leg to the front binding

lift track – the smooth path under a *surface lift* where skis and snowboards glide along en route to the top

linking – putting isolated turns together, switching from heel to toe to heel without stopping

moguls – bumps that form naturally on ungroomed slopes

nose – the front tip of the board

ollie – getting air without a jump or increasing the amount of air by loading up weight on the *tail* and then springing off the nose, like a sideward jump

phat air – huge, high, dangerous or stylish air. Also known as "big air"

pipe – shortened form of *halfpipe*

pivoting – turning/sliding/steering the board

plate bindings – binding system compatible with *hard boots* and a *carving* board

poach – to illegally take advantage of fresh *powder* or a park feature that has been closed or roped off by the resort, usually for safety reasons

pow/powder – fresh, untouched snowfall, hopefully deep and light

pumping – using your legs to generate up and down momentum for bigger *air* in the *pipe*

regular – stance with the right leg in back and the left leg in front (see *goofy*)

revert – to switch stance from *fakie* to forward or forward to *fakie* while the board is on the snow

scootching – getting around a flat area with both bindings attached by sliding the hips forward, then pulling the board along using the leg muscles

sideslipping – controlling the *edge angle* of a snowboard that is perpendicular to the *fall line* to slow down, speed up or stop

skate – pushing the snowboard along the snow while one foot is attached to the board; the method of locomotion for gliding in the *flats*

sketching – *skidding* out of a turn or landing instead of using the edge to control it

skidding – sliding instead of *carving* a turn

slope – a trail or hill that one snowboards on, or the steepness of that trail

slopestyle competition – a *freestyle* event in which each rider is judged on performance of a series of tricks

soft boots – the most widely used *freestyle* boot, made of flexible, waterproof, insulated materials

stance – the placement of the bindings on the snowboard which determines the angles and width of the feet and distribution of weight for the rider

step-in binding – binding systems that have been developed for both *hard* and *soft boots* which allow the rider to step into the binding without bending over or sitting down to adjust straps

stomp pad – a grippy resting place on top of the snowboard for the back foot when it is out of the binding

strap binding – the most widely used binding, consisting of a toe and heel strap that must be attached and adjusted, and a *highback*

surface lift – lifts that pull the rider uphill while the board remains on the snow

switch stance – riding *fakie* or backwards

tail – the rear tip of the snowboard

tail roll – sliding or spinning off the *tail* of the board

terrain park – area in a resort set aside for *freestyle* riders and skiers, with manmade snow features such as jumps, berms, rails, rollers, quarterpipes and *halfpipes*

toe edge – the edge of the snowboard that is closest to the toes

toeside – a turn, takeoff or landing that is on the *toe edge*

traverse – to move diagonally across a hill

traverse sideslip – to direct a board across a *fall line* while continuing to *sideslip* downhill to adjust balance; see *falling leaf sideslip*

tweaking – to stretch out a move to its most stylish point

twin tip – a *freestyle* board with identical nose and tail, designed to ride *fakie* and forward with equal ease

unweighting – jumping upward through extension of the knees and ankles to relieve the board of the pressure of gravity

wrist guards – snowboard-specific protective braces that fit inside or are built into gloves to prevent wrist fractures

Before you ride

It's crucial that your first experience on a snowboard is a great one. Snowboarding has a reputation of being difficult on the first day, but with some expert guidance and tips to prepare you physically and mentally your chances of a successful first snowboard mission will increase immeasurably.

TAKE A LESSON!

For everyone's sake as well as your own, your first snowboarding experience should be under the guidance of a qualified instructor. When combined with the advice and techniques offered in this book, a professional lesson with a qualified snowboard instructor ensures that your first experience is an enjoyable one. Your friends mean well when they offer you a free lesson, but for your first time on a snowboard, spend the money and save yourself some frustration and bruises—and maybe a friendship.

Some basic first-day instruction will have you beginning to ride downhill under control and before long the bug will bite and you'll be crazy for snowboarding. Do-it-yourself snowboard lessons can end up being very expensive if you wind up in the x-ray department. Once you learn the basics of controlling speed and steering, lessons are not that critical, but for the first day, sign up.

❄ KIDS AND SNOWBOARDING ❄

Kids think learning to snowboard is cool. A kid will wake up early on a weekend, give the instructor undivided attention and take face plant after face plant with a smile just to learn to snowboard. No doubt about it, snowboarding has a cool image with kids, so you usually don't have to sell them on the idea.

But don't tell them it's good for them. Modern kids need active sports: they spend too much of their leisure time playing sports with their thumbs in front of a computer screen.

Learning to ride builds muscles, confidence, self-esteem and grace in a youngster. Becoming a skilled rider has nothing to do with size or aggression. In fact, it is one of the few sports in which size doesn't matter and that encourages creativity and individualism, while allowing a kid to work on his/her own level without fear of comparison or ridicule. Given a good first-day experience, very few kids don't take to snowboarding.

PRO TIP

Alex Allen
Professional snowboard instructor, Arapahoe Basin, Colorado

"Most snowboard schools will ask that your child be at least seven or eight years old to try snowboarding. I'm not saying that a five-year-old can't learn to snowboard; he or she will just need more time and attention, and will require one-to-one instruction. On a snowboard, a child must use both legs to balance on one edge, and that takes more advanced coordination than skiing. I recommend letting kids ski for a few years first. This will allow them to acquire the basics of sliding on snow and chairlifts."

USING YOUR HEAD TO RIDE BETTER

The most important thing to bring to snowboarding is a positive attitude. The mind is a powerful force and can affect how you perceive the challenge ahead. Whether you are strapping into your boots for the first time or getting your first air, thinking only positive thoughts will help you succeed.

Fear can be an obstacle to learning to ride a snowboard, even if you are an extremely cool dude. By thinking powerful, positive thoughts you can help banish your fears and embrace the thrilling new challenges that await you!

This may sound corny, but it really works. Relax, take some deep breaths and repeat the following words to yourself:

"This is going to be fun."

"I'm well prepared. I'll be fine."

"Hey, relax, it's only snowboarding."

"Snowboarding is a great way to stay in shape and have some fun with my kids."

Conquering something gives you a feeling of confidence that overflows into all aspects of your life. If you can steer a snowboard across a snowy slope with the wind in your face on your first day, what else is beyond your mastery? Bring 'em on!

The fact is we learn much better when we are relaxed. The body is less stiff and better prepared to react to the terrain and to other moving people. Deep breathing helps to calm even the most frazzled mind and by conquering initial anxieties, a new rider can better focus on the instructor's words and demonstrations.

Mental visualization is a technique used by top athletes to accomplish new feats. Watch snowboarding videos and imagine yourself doing the same thing. Imagine yourself in one of the pictures in this book. Replay a movie of yourself linking perfect turns over and over in your mind, including as many small details as possible, or try your hand at snowboarding computer games. When it comes time to actually try turning, the brain will remember, and your body will execute it. Relax, think positively, imagine it and it will happen.

FUEL UP

The first day on a snowboard is the most demanding. Snowboarding is a very simple movement of switching edges from toe to heel to toe, but getting to that point requires concentration and a great deal of energy. Expect to be exhausted by noon.

Start the morning off with a nutritious breakfast and plenty of fluids. Avoid drinking alcohol the night before, as this will dehydrate you and hungover is no way to learn a strenuous, new sport.

Bring a bottle of water with you to the lesson and stash it somewhere nearby. Bring along an energy bar and put it somewhere other than your back pocket so that it doesn't turn to dust. Choose an energy bar that will not freeze solid and rearrange your dental work.

PRO TIP

EATING TO RIDE

Jewels Larsen
Extreme competition specialist and all-around expert backcountry rider

"Most of the time, riders do not even think about what they are eating before, during, or after they ride. But try to keep track and watch what you eat and you will see the difference.

Start when you first wake up with at least 1 glass of water or herbal tea before ingesting anything at all. You need to flush your body of any extra waste in your system first thing! Breakfast is exactly what it says: breaking your fast. Fruits and fruit juice are excellent for this fast-breaking and to assist in flushing your body out. Most of us need a bit more sustenance to hold us over until lunch, so this is when cereal, oatmeal, toast or bagel is good to eat. Those little packages of instant oatmeal are awesome for a quick breakfast. I make 2 packets for my breakfast and that usually holds me over until at least mid-morning or lunch. Yogurt and granola is another great combination that is good for you and fills you up without weighing you down.

Eating nothing is not a very good option, as usually your body does not have fuel in order to have the most fun and ride your best. Heavier foods like eggs, hash browns, pancakes, bacon and sausage will probably just drag you down with grease and sugar.

After breakfast, put together a lightweight lunch to carry to the hill. I prefer a peanut butter and jelly or a ham and cheese sandwich. Both are good energy foods and will not make you feel like taking a nap. I always include an apple or some grapes and also a small bag of pretzels or chips. The salt will actually benefit your body and help you maintain your hydration level.

Find an energy bar that you enjoy. These bars are nutritious and fuel you up until you can get a meal. When the hunger pains hit and you still want a few more powder runs, you can pull one out of your pocket and munch away while resting on a chairlift ride.

Finally, after a full day of riding powder, hiking the pipe, or racing your friends through the trees, a good well-rounded dinner is a great way to replenish your body's lost nutrients and help you rest much better at night."

DRESS FOR SUCCESS

Warm, dry and comfortable is the best way to learn something new. Dressing in three or more layers gives you lots of options if you start to overheat or if bad weather moves in. The inside layer should be stretchy and should draw sweat away from the skin while providing some warmth. Natural fibers like cotton or wool feel good until they get wet and stay wet. Polyester fabrics, such as long johns, that wick moisture from the skin and dry quickly are much more comfortable for long days in the snow. Denim jeans? In one word: NO.

PILE ON THE LAYERS Socks are the most important inner layer and the key to a good boot fit. Choose thinner over thicker, so the feet won't be slipping around in the socks. Cold feet are usually the result of cramped feet and no air circulation, not lack of insulation. Socks need to come at least halfway up the calf and no other piece of clothing should be stuffed into the boot, just the sock and the ankle.

For the middle layer, fleece is lightweight and traps warm air next to the body. This layer can be taken on or off depending on the temperature and the amount of activity. Stash a fleece neck gaiter in a pocket in case the wind comes up or it starts to snow.

On the outside, wear a windproof/waterproof layer, preferably padded or reinforced in the seat and knees, and roomy enough to allow for lots of freedom of movement. One-piece ski suits are not recommended, because you will have to crouch down often to strap in bindings.

You don't need to go out and buy a whole new snowboarding outfit to try this sport. Any rugged fabric that keeps you warm, dry and padded will be fine. Chances are you won't be looking all that cool at first, anyway.

Gloves should be made with a durable, waterproof material, as your hands will be touching the snow quite frequently while learning to snowboard. They should have tall cuffs to stop snow entering and they should be easy to slip on and off.

CRUCIAL EYEWEAR Sunglasses seem like a great idea until your first face plant. Secure goggles protect the eyes from UV rays, snow, wind and tree branches, so stash your sunglasses in a pocket for later.

Your eyes need serious protection against sunlight reflecting off the snow. Almost all goggles provide 100% UV protection, but certain tints are better for certain light conditions. On cloudy or flat-light days or for night riding, clear, rose or persimmon lenses are the best choice. For sunny days, bronze is the best choice. If you can't afford two pairs of goggles, choose an all-conditions color such as rose or light orange with a bronze finish. Outer finishes are cosmetic (and look cool), but also offer a darker tint to the lens. Another option is to buy goggles that come with interchangeable lenses.

Double lens goggles with good ventilation are best for preventing fog. Bring a few tissues or a cloth for wiping snow or fog from the goggles and store them in a carrying case when not using them to avoid damage.

LAYERING

Perspiration

Waterproof shell

Synthetic or down parka

Fleece jacket or vest

Synthetic or wool shirt and pants

Synthetic wicking long johns

Heat

Skin

Wrist fractures are the most common injury for beginner snowboarders. Snowboard-specific wrist guards, which are stiff braces that fit inside or are built into gloves, cut the risk of fractures. Be sure that your gloves are easy to get on and off, as you will need bare hands for some tasks. Wrist guards made for inline skating are not as effective in preventing snowboarding injuries.

HELMETS Protective headgear makes sense for all levels of riders, all the time. With high-speed quad and six-pack lifts whisking large numbers of people to the top, the slopes are becoming more crowded. Well-groomed slopes and high-tech equipment make faster speeds easier and collisions are becoming more common. It doesn't take much for a collision to result in a concussion or worse, so be kind to your gray matter and wear a brain bucket.

For those of us without 20/20 vision there are added complications. For contact lens wearers, goggles are a must because wind dries out the eyes and because if a lens blinks out, it can usually be found in the goggles. Those who prefer conventional prescription eyeglasses will need to find a pair of goggles that fit over them comfortably. This usually means a higher-volume pair that will sacrifice its aerodynamic and lightweight features somewhat. But you have to see well to ride safely.

Most competitions require helmets, and the pros and serious competitors set an example (and a fashion statement) for the rest of us. Helmets are becoming more commonplace every year and improvements in design have made them less bulky, more stylish and better ventilated. If you choose to spend extra money on the best equipment, this is where to do it.

Many resorts are located at high altitude where the sun's rays are intensified by the thin air. Even if it's an overcast day, make sure all exposed areas are protected with at least 30 SPF waterproof sunscreen, not forgetting the tops of ears.

PROTECTIVE GEAR Hip pads can be rented for the first few days of learning to snowboard to cushion falls and keep your seat warm and dry. They are stretchy and pull on like bike shorts and are lined with extra padding in the backside to prevent tailbone bruises. Even pro riders use hip pads when trying new moves in the halfpipe and terrain park. Knee pads can also be worn between long underwear and pants.

The warmest and most protective style is a full helmet. Chop helmets do not come down as far on the head and offer better vision and hearing and less bulk. Park-style helmets are more like skateboard helmets with lots of vent holes and no insulation. These are more popular with halfpipe and terrain park riders who don't usually experience the wind chill of high speeds.

STRETCHING

Being flexible makes snowboarding easier, whether it's strapping into bindings or tweaking out big air. Flexibility doesn't happen overnight, but it's one of the few attributes that can actually improve with age. You're never too old to work on your flexibility, and you will never be flexible enough. So, don't just stand there—stretch whenever and wherever you can!

Stretch after warming up, because cold muscles aren't very pliable and so risk injury. Deep lunges work well to raise body temperature, as does walking uphill or jumping on the spot. Usually the walk from your car to the lift, carrying your equipment, will warm you up.

When muscles are warm, hold stretches for 15 to 30 seconds, and never bounce. Quadriceps and hamstring muscles will be doing most of the workload, so any chance during the day to stretch them will help ease muscle soreness at the end of the day.

You don't have to be in a yoga studio to stretch. Waiting in the lift line is a good time to roll your neck side to side or stretch out the quadriceps by pulling the heel toward the buttocks. If you are in the cafeteria, waiting for the rest of your group to finish lunch, put your foot up on a chair and stretch the hamstrings.

If you sneak in stretches all day long, you won't feel like you must stop everything and stretch first thing in the morning. If you ride with friends and family, you will always find moments perfect for stretching.

ARE YOU FIT TO RIDE?

Humans are not built for snowboarding. Our joints evolved to perform a variety of movements and our muscles evolved to be equally strong in all parts of the body. Our ancestors had to climb, leap, run and swing to find food or avoid danger, but rarely did they encounter the jarring and twisting falls of snow sports.

To make matters worse, modern man spends hours driving a car or working at a computer to put food on the table, which leaves the muscles even less prepared for snowboarding. To succeed in snowboarding special attention must be paid to increasing lung capacity and strengthening the muscles attached to the joints. A well conditioned body has a reduced chance of injury. Keeping your body in good shape year-round will decrease your chances of becoming an injury statistic when you hit the slopes.

AEROBIC TRAINING Most people think that riding keeps them in shape, but the chairlift takes away much of the cardiovascular training. Aerobic conditioning is needed to prevent injuries that occur because of fatigue. Having aerobic energy reserves can mean the difference between a clean mogul run and having to sit down and catch your breath every five turns.

Any type of aerobic activity is fine, but to avoid burn out, the more variety the better—dance or aerobic exercise

PRO TIP

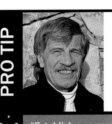

MAKE IT FUN

John Gillingham

Professional exercise instructor, fitness consultant, skier and snowboarder

"Establish a year-round fitness program and fine-tune it several weeks before you start snowboarding. Boarding is primarily an "anaerobic" activity: short bursts of intensity followed by a rest period to catch your breath. Establish a good aerobic base—run, walk, swim, inline skate, crosstrain—and do it at a low level of intensity for a long duration (minimum 30 to 40 minutes). Add anaerobic activities (high-intensity activities for one to two minutes) such as sprints, running stairs, jumping rope, or any other activity that makes you huff and puff similar to when you ride.

Making your cardiovascular program fun is absolutely a must! If it isn't fun, you won't stick with it. Find a buddy to do it with, be consistent and crosstrain from one activity to another.

The final part of your program is to stretch, stretch and stretch some more. Stretch after your warm-up and workout instead of at the beginning when muscles are cold."

classes, tennis, swimming, cycling and jogging are just a few examples. Too much of one sport can cause imbalances in opposing muscle groups, leaving a joint ripe for injury. So, mix it up and keep it fun, and you will be less likely to slack off or quit training.

STRENGTH TRAINING Strengthening the calf, quadricep and hamstring muscles through aerobic sports and weightlifting can strengthen the knees in preparation for the impact of landings. High repetitions of squats and half-squats done with low weight closely simulates snowboarding. Don't drop below a 90-degree angle in your knees, and keep your knees aligned over your ankles, not your toes. Do an extra set in your snowboard stance.

Various lower-body weight machines are also great for building stronger knees, but keep the weight low and make sure to maintain correct form.

CORE STRENGTH   "Core strength" is the hottest buzzword in fitness today. Devotees of all sports are realizing that the torso is the foundation of the body, and that the arms and legs are really extensions of the trunk. Strong core muscles (abdomen, back and trunk) make every move more efficient, from tight turns in the bumps to bigger air in the pipe.

The old-fashioned way to strengthen core muscles is abdominal curls and crunches, but do equal amounts of lower back exercises too. The "Superman" is a simple way to work the lower back. Lie on your stomach and lift your arms and legs simultaneously, building up to as many repetitions as you can. Hold a few of them for five seconds.

Fitness balls are becoming popular for toning and stretching all parts of the body, but are especially helpful in developing core strength and balance for everyone

from weekend warriors to pro athletes. The rolling motion strengthens core muscles and promotes better posture. In fact, just sitting on a fitness ball instead of an office chair burns 10% more energy and strengthens the abdominal and lower back muscles.

UPPER BODY

The joints of the wrists, elbows and shoulders are especially prone to injuries caused by jarring falls. Building up strength and flexibility in the upper body is no guarantee against rips or dislocations, but it definitely helps your chances. Snowboarding does not work the upper body very much, so participate in sports that compensate for this, like wakeboarding, nordic skiing, kayaking and rock climbing.

BALANCE AND COORDINATION

Snowboarding demands quick reflexes. Your muscles must be able to respond and land in any direction. Instead of just jogging, run backwards, sideways, and around trees. Your neighbors may give you a weird look, but they were already wondering when they saw you bouncing on the fitness ball.

In the gym, try single-leg balances and single-leg squats with your eyes closed. If self-training fails, check into yoga or tai chi classes. Bongo boards, hula hoops, skateboards and pogo sticks can add some fun and aerobics to balance training.

HYDRATION

Riding a snowboard under the influence of alcohol is as dangerous as driving a car when drunk. Alcohol slows down your reflexes, impairs your judgment and robs your body of warmth and water. It really does nothing positive for your snowboarding, so reach for the water instead.

Your body needs water more than any other nutrient to perform well on the slopes. Many riders are seeing the correlation between water intake and athletic potential, and are carrying water bottles, or portable hydration systems on their backs.

Getting your equipment "dialed"

Getting your equipment "dialed" from day one is vital to your success. Instruction time is precious and your learning curve is steep, so you want to avoid trudging back to the rental shop because the bindings aren't adjusted correctly or the boots don't fit. If you buy a board or borrow one from a friend, have a professional set the bindings for you and show you how to use them. It only takes a few minutes but it saves lots of valuable time. The more familiar you feel with your equipment from the start, the more attention you'll be able to devote to learning to ride.

THE BASIC FREESTYLE SET-UP

Basic freestyle boards are recommended for beginner riders. These boards have similar or twin tips, which means that the nose and tail are almost identical in width. This style of board makes it equally comfortable for the rider to lead downhill with either the nose or the tail, an essential skill in learning to steer the board.

The easiest way to differentiate between the nose and tail is to look at how the bindings are mounted. The back binding (closest to the tail of the board) will point straight toward the toe edge of the board while the front binding (closest to the nose of the board) will point slightly toward the nose.

A clip leash (above) or Velcro leash (right) help solve the problem of runaway boards, and are a requirement at most ski resorts.

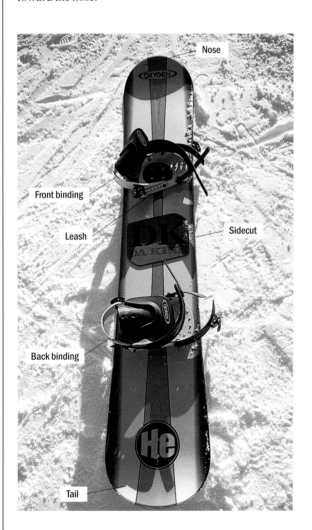

Nose

Front binding

Leash

Sidecut

Back binding

Tail

Sidecut is the amount of curve along the edges of the board. It is the difference in width between the nose and tail, and the waist, the narrowest portion of the board. Sidecut affects the width of turns: more sidecut produces wider turns; less sidecut produces narrower turns.

At first, snowboarding borrowed technology from skiing by adapting metal edges, P-Tex bases and wood cores, but these days snowboarding has left its mark on alpine and telemark skiing, as both have benefitted from snowboard research and technology. The hourglass-shaped ski is the new rage because it's easier to turn, floats more in powder and is quicker in the bumps. The ski design was borrowed from the sidecut of snowboards.

On a beginner's board, it may be difficult at first to distinguish the nose from the tail. It is especially difficult with lower-profile step-in bindings, which look almost the same at heel and toe. A handy way to locate the nose of the board is to find the leash, a strap with a clip or Velcro attachment system at the end that secures the board to the rider's front foot, or ankle or calf. Leashes are required for riders to board the chairlifts at most mountain resorts, so make sure the board you are using has one.

BOOTS   The most important piece of equipment to get dialed are the boots, as you need the maximum control possible out there on the slopes. The boots transfer energy from the feet to the board, so if the boots are too large, there will be "energy leaks." These leaks cause certain muscles to work extra hard, resulting in cramps and fatigue. Boot pain is something to avoid so make sure you get the right fit from the beginning.

Take your time when trying on boots and take with you the socks you will ride in. Lace the boots tight and buckle them down as tight as they will be when you are riding. If it hurts a little somewhere, it will be killing you after a few hours. Ask to try on other sizes and brands. Different brands fit different types of feet, so shop around.

Step-in boots should have a sturdy ankle strap attached to the boot that holds down the heel, especially when applying pressure to the toe edge. This strap will need to withstand quite a bit of pressure, especially for larger riders, so avoid Velcro arrangements and opt for a wide plastic ratchet strap if possible.

When trying on boots, place the board flat on the shop floor and strap in or step into the bindings with both feet (see page 24–25). When the bindings are snug, lean forward against a counter or wall and bend your knees (see page 21). Your heels should not move inside your boots. If there is lots of play in the heel, that is, if the boot lifts up when leaning forward (or performing a "heel lift"), then tighten up the laces and buckles or try on a smaller size boot.

Step-in bindings (below left) put all the force of the turn into the boot. Ensure the binding has a wide adjustable strap to keep the heel snug. Boots that are designed for strap bindings (below) also need to have a snug fit. Opt for those with adjustable inner linings.

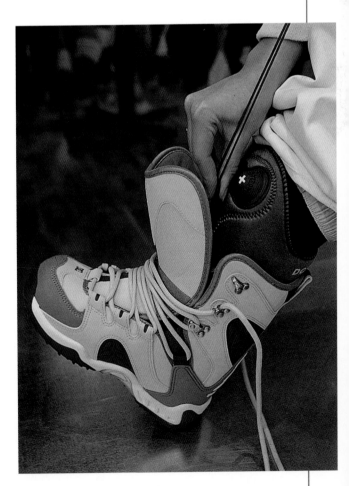

BINDINGS

Snowboard binding systems are like snowflakes; no two are exactly alike, but they all have the same basic function of securing the foot to the snowboard. Most bindings fall into two categories: strap or step-ins, with or without highbacks.

STRAP BINDINGS The original and still bestselling snowboard binding is the strap system. Strap bindings are comfortable, adjustable and very secure, and models have become lighter and stronger as snowboard technology has advanced.

The best strap bindings have ample amounts of wide padding at the ankle and toe straps. The tops of your feet will be taking some pressure when you learn to edge, so avoid wimpy straps!

1. Place your front foot in the front binding. Make sure your heel is positioned securely against the highback.

2. Secure the ankle strap first, tightening as snug as possible without pain. Then secure the toe strap in the same way.

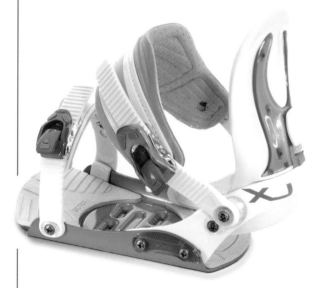

3. Place your back foot in the back binding. Tighten the ankle and toe straps down to a firm hold.

Strap bindings also feature slap-ratchet systems that make it a breeze to feed the ladder strap and click down to the perfect amount of tightness. Strap bindings do have a tendency to loosen up at the major stress areas, so check to make sure that all screws are tight and all four straps are accounted for.

STEP-IN BINDINGS Step-in binding systems have become very popular with rental shops because they (usually) give the first-time rider fewer gadgets to fuss with. On a level surface, a rider can step into the binding without leaning down or sitting down to get "strapped in." Thus, they afford a little more dignity, are more familiar to skiers, and avoid wet-seat syndrome!

1. On a clicker step-in binding, the toe steps in first.

2. The heel then presses down to lock the boot and binding in place.

3. The leash on the front binding attaches to your front boot or around the ankle.

Riders who prefer straps or step-ins will argue that one is better than the other, but it usually comes down to personal preference and finding the right boot first. On snowy days, step-ins can get clogged with snow or ice that has to be pounded out with a screwdriver or ski pole (be nice to skiers, you may need them one day). Straps offer more adjustments, so you can tighten them on icy days and loosen them for soft snow. Regardless of which type of binding system you end up with, don't head for the slopes until you know exactly how to get in and out of them!

THE HIGHBACK The highback is the large curved piece of plastic screwed to the base of the binding. Highbacks are found on all bindings or are built into the boot with some step-in systems. The invention of the highback gave riders some control (leverage) over their heel edge. On toe turns, a rider can adjust the amount of pressure that the edge puts against the snow by flexion of the ankles, but on heel turns, the ankle cannot flex backward. The rider's calves lean back against the highback on heel turns, and this helps bring the toes up with very little effort for more edge control.

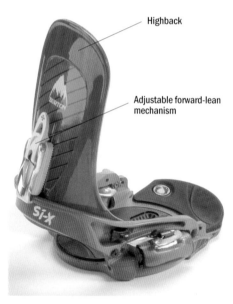

Highback

Adjustable forward-lean mechanism

ADJUSTING YOUR OWN BINDINGS Mountain resorts are becoming more snowboard-friendly. In lift lines metal rails are replacing ropes to give riders the support and push that ski poles provide. Some resorts provide benches at the top of lifts for riders to sit down and strap in. Tool stations are often provided, with screwdrivers, wrenches and a counter to work on.

Until snowboard bindings are perfected, the screws, nuts and bolts that hold the highest stress areas together will tend to loosen up with everyday use. They need to be

Always carry a snowboard tool with you when you ride and experiment with different angles.

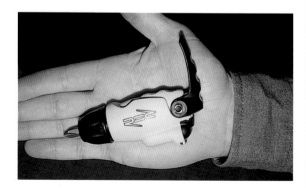

❄ STANCE—ARE YOU REGULAR OR GOOFY? ❄

The majority of riders are regular-footed. That is, they ride with their right foot at the back. But there are a sizable number of riders who are goofy, and ride with their left foot back. If you have done a sideways sport before, such as skateboarding, surfing or wakeboarding, then you will already have a preference.

When you first learn to ride, you will be required to ride both ways, and you may discover that you prefer one stance over the other, but it's not that critical. Bindings can be adjusted quickly, and this can be done right on the slopes.

Every well-rounded rider will learn to ride fakie (backwards), so you will eventually learn both stances. But at first, put your strong leg in back to do the steering. If you kick a soccer ball with your left leg or throw with your left arm, then you are probably goofy. If you begin cartwheels with your right leg or swing a tennis racket with your right arm, then you are probably regular. You could be right-handed and left-footed. It's not an exact science and it won't create permanent psychological trauma if you end up with the "wrong" stance. Most brains can learn to turn goofy or regular, but if you feel that you must change your stance, it can be done right on the slopes with a snowboard tool, a palm-size life saver that has multiple functions.

tightened regularly to ensure that a strap doesn't fall off and get lost, or the binding isn't ripped off the board by the forces of gravity during a turn.

Not every mountain resort provides tool stations, however, so have a snowboard tool in your pocket at all times. A snowboard tool is a small investment that will pay off over years of riding.

Snowboards and bindings have become practically universal in compatibility, allowing any brand of binding to be interchanged and adjusted on any brand of snowboard. With the standardized insert pattern of snowboards, mounting and adjusting bindings has become simple and something that even the technologically-challenged can master.

Most beginners start with a stance of about shoulder width and angles of about 15 degrees on the front binding and 3 degrees on the back. The disc that fits inside the base plate has teeth that click into angle increments. Point the disc arrow toward the desired angle degree, screw in all four screws and you are ready to rip.

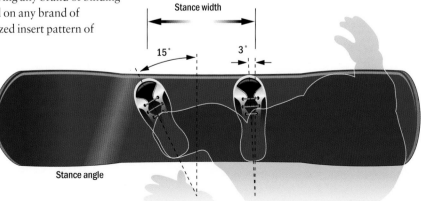

Stance width

15°   3°

Stance angle

CHAPTER THREE

Getting from here to there (or skating ...)

A snowboard plus gravity will take you from the top of the hill to the bottom, but getting through lift lines and across flat areas takes some effort and finesse. Before even considering getting on a chairlift, perfect your skating and stopping skills on a gentle incline with lots of room to turn.

A runaway snowboard can gain speed quickly and become a deadly weapon! (which is why most resorts require a leash.) When resting a board on the snow, place the board with bindings facing down so that it won't take an unscheduled descent without you (*see above*).

When putting on the board, attach the leash first, then step or strap into the front binding. The front foot should be pointing toward the toe edge but 5 to 15 degrees slightly forward (*see page 27*).

BOARD BASICS

Acclimatize yourself to the board by using your free foot (back leg) as a base of support, picking up the board and swinging it back, forth and around (1–2). Feel its weight, length, and width while making sure the toe and ankle straps are buckled tight. Stomp the board on the snow a few times. Change direction by picking up the board, turning it 180 degrees, placing it on the snow and lifting your back leg around to the other side of the board (2–3).

Place the back leg behind the heel edge and pull the toe edge of the board up with the front foot. Feel the heel edge and press against it (4).

Now, step in front of the toe edge and lift the heel of the front foot. Feel the toe edge of the snowboard pressing against the snow (5).

PIVOTING YOUR BACK FOOT

Place your back foot on the board, up against the back binding (**1**). Some boards have a foam or rubber stomp pad in front of the back binding, which is used for traction. Frequently, rental boards do not have a stomp pad and this will make the board a little more slippery to stand on.

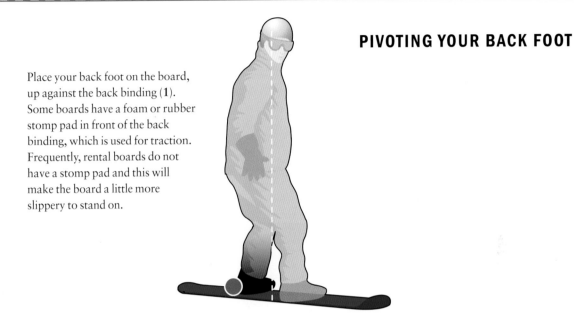

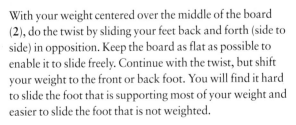

With your weight centered over the middle of the board (**2**), do the twist by sliding your feet back and forth (side to side) in opposition. Keep the board as flat as possible to enable it to slide freely. Continue with the twist, but shift your weight to the front or back foot. You will find it hard to slide the foot that is supporting most of your weight and easier to slide the foot that is not weighted.

Shift the weight forward and slide your back leg from side to side (**3**). When you begin to make your first turns, it will be critical to keep your weight shifted forward so that your back leg is free to pivot and steer the board. The number one problem new riders share is leaning back in fear. When your weight is shifted back, the back leg cannot pivot, and you essentially disconnect the steering mechanism of the board.

SKATING

Learning to skate is essential to getting on and off the lifts and traveling around on flat or slightly inclined terrain. The hardest thing to get used to is traveling in the direction that the board's nose is pointing while the front foot is pointing sideways. Add the fact that the back leg pushes off while pointing towards the nose of the board, and you have an awkward, pigeon-toed stance. Unless you are an alien from another planet where beings naturally slide sideways to travel, this will not feel normal. It should feel downright weird, though if you have skateboarded, this will feel less strange. Yes, you will be traveling, say, north, but your front foot will be pointing northeast (or northwest if you are goofy). So sliding around on a board in this fashion will feel quite odd at first. You will trip a few times and feel a little foolish, even if you have skateboarding experience.

STAY CENTERED!

Imagine the very center of your mass as just inside your navel. If this part of your body is centered over the board, all the other body parts can relax and perform well, but if your rear is not over the board, then you will have to wave your arms frantically to compensate for the imbalance. Bend up and down in your knees and ankles, not in your waist. If you are centered over the board, every aspect of snowboarding will be easier to learn.

Keep the board flat to the snow and pointing in the direction of travel (**1**). Keep your weight over the front foot so that the back foot is free to push, and keep the back foot close to the bindings when pushing off the snow (**2–3**). If the back foot gets too far away from your center of balance (the front foot), then you will be traveling in two different directions, which is impossible, so you will either fall forward or do the splits, neither of which is all that fun.

Do small push-offs at first and increase the amount of push from the back leg as you gain confidence. Try pushing from your heel side, too. Anytime you are sliding forward, take a break and rest the back foot on the board in front of the back binding. Free ride! Energy saver!

PUSH FROM TOE SIDE

When starting to skate you can push with the back foot from either toe or heel side. Keep your weight centered, look where you want to go, and take comfortable strides. For toe side skating start with small steps and tilt the board slightly on its toe edge (**1**). The movement you make is similar to pushing off with a child's scooter (**2**).

PUSH FROM HEEL SIDE

For heel side skating tilt the board slightly on its heel edge (**3**) and use the same scooterlike movement as you did for the toe side skate (**4**).

If the terrain is slightly uphill, then smaller and more frequent pushes, as well as more energy, will be required. If the terrain becomes too steep, skating becomes an inefficient means of

travel. Face the hill, tilt onto the toe edge so that it digs into the snow (**1**), and stair-step uphill with the free foot leading and the front foot and snowboard trailing (**2**).

Anytime you are resting, use your free foot as an anchor and engage an edge for extra stability. If you need to rest while facing uphill, then engage your toe edge and use the back foot as an anchor.

STRAIGHT GLIDES

Straight glides are the first real experience of snowboarding! This aspect of your snowboard education is extremely tiring, because to practice each glide requires a climb uphill.

Find a gentle slope with lots of flat run-out space at the bottom and as little traffic as possible. Skate uphill a short distance, say ten yards (10m), and lift the board around so it points downhill, using your free foot as an anchor on the snow (1-4). When you are ready and the coast is clear, step on the board just in front of the back binding (5, **opposite**). Stay centered and loose. Look where you want to go, not at the snowboard. Let gravity do its thing—COAST!

You will immediately realize the importance of a stopping mechanism. Learning to turn out of a glide will enable you to unload from a chairlift in control. First-timers who get on the chairlift before mastering this skill risk breaking their wrists when they fall backward getting off the lift. Once you can stand tall on a board and glide down an incline, turning whichever way the situation dictates, then you are ready for the chairlift.

5

Your first descents should be on gentle, quiet, groomed slopes with plenty of flat run-out space, so that you can get used to gliding without worrying about how you will stop.

HEEL-TURNS

Most new riders find heel-turns easier to learn than toe-turns. It's purely psychological. The mind likes facing downhill in the direction of travel better than it likes facing uphill while the body is traveling downhill. Eventually both turns will feel equally good. (No, make that GREAT.)

Skate uphill a little farther this time. Glide downhill with your board flat to the snow, then begin to press the heel edge and lift the toes (**1**). Look ahead and point with your leading arm in the direction you are turning. Keep your knees slightly bent and press gently into the snow with your heel edge (**2**). Take a wide slow turn and let the board slide on the heel edge to a stop (**3**). Step off with the free leg and wave to the cheering crowds. You have just tested the brakes and gas pedal of your snowboard: when the board is sideways and pressing an edge into the hill, it stops; when the board is flat to the snow or pointed downhill, it accelerates.

The fall line is the most direct route to the bottom of a hill and the way a ball or a stream would travel due to gravity. When the board is perpendicular to the fall line with an edge engaged, it will stop.

You are learning to trust your edges. It's hard to believe at first that pressing the heels or toes into the snow will steer and stop the board, but as you experiment with your first turns, you will realize (and for some of us, realize slowly and reluctantly) that these darn edges work! Sliding the board sideways and pressing your heels into the snow is a much easier way to stop than crashing. It's been proven!

GLIDING INTO A TOE-TURN

Stand tall and centered on the board. Look and point in the direction you are headed with your leading arm, and keep your knees slightly bent (**1**). When you are ready to turn, gradually slide the board sideways and press your toes into the snow (**2–3**). When the turn is finished, you

will be facing uphill (**4**). Step off the board to maintain balance after stopping. It sounds easy, but it may take quite a few climbs uphill to practice this skill. This is the most exhausting and sometimes discouraging part of the first lesson. Hang in there!

TROUBLESHOOTING

PROBLEM: Going faster in the turn instead of slowing down.

SOLUTION: If you dig the edge into the snow too hard or too soon, a quick carved turn will result. Save that for a later lesson. Start the tail of the board pivoting first, then press your heels or toes gently and gradually slide to a stop.

3

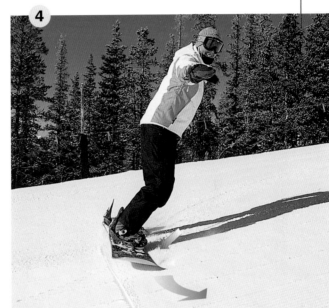

4

TROUBLESHOOTING

PROBLEM: Leaning back, accelerating, can't get board around, weight on back leg?

SOLUTION: Remember when you were doing the twist? (see page 31). That back leg must be free to slide, so keep your weight forward and your mindset firmly downhill.

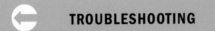

MASTERING THE CHAIRLIFT

You are ready for a chairlift when you can slide down an incline and perform a toe-turn or a heel-turn, depending on the terrain, and can take evasive action when people happen to fall in front of you. After skating uphill so many times to practice gliding, you will gain a new appreciation for a chairlift. Riding a chairlift for the first time might seem nerve-wracking but any anticipation you feel should disappear after a few rides.

Detachable high-speed lifts, trams and gondolas are the easiest lifts for beginners to get on and off. There's plenty of time to get in place when loading and get out of the way when unloading. Detachable high-speed chairlifts usually have a wide, gentle run-off, and the rider can simply stand up and skate away.

Traditional chairlifts do not slow down when loading and unloading, but the lift attendant can slow down the entire lift for a first-timer. Watch from the lift line and study other riders, particularly ones with the same stance, getting on the lift. Do the same thing at the top of the hill if you have difficulty getting off.

UPWARDLY MOBILE

Keep your snowboard pointed straight ahead and flat to the snow while in the lift line (**1**). Skate up to the loading zone, look back at the oncoming chair, and sit down as the chairlift nears the back of your knees (**2**). Keep your board flat, especially when you first sit down on the chairlift (**3**). If the board gets sideways or tilted, it can catch in the snow before the chair takes you up and out of the loading zone and you'll risk injuring yourself. Once the chair is a few feet in the air, you can relax and let the board hang.

If the chair has a safety bar, pull that down. (Some resorts require it.) The most snowboarder-friendly bars have a foot rest, which eases the strain of the snowboard weight on the attached foot. If the bar doesn't have a foot rest, tuck your free foot underneath your board to help support its weight (**see main picture, left**).

If you are sharing a chair with a rider of the opposite stance, line up for the chair facing each other to minimize contact of the boards. This also makes it easier to talk on the ride up and see each other while gliding down the unloading ramp (**4**). If you happen to get on a chair with your back to the other rider, you can still unload safely. Just be sure to turn away from each other, toward the outside.

If your chairlift partner is also new to lifts, remind each other as you are reaching the top to point the board straight ahead. Lift the safety bar as you near the last lift tower (**5, opposite**).

As the chair arrives at the top of the ramp, let the board land flat to the snow and plant your free foot on the board (**6**). Push off the chair with your hands as you stand up tall and centered. Ride the ramp straight down, like the straight glide you practiced earlier. Keep the board flat to the snow and don't engage an edge or even think about turning until you are off the ramp and in a wider, flatter area (**7**). Then make a controlled heel- or toe-turn to a stop, step off the board with your free foot and skate away.

Get the heck out of there! Even if you fall or get tangled up, untangle yourself and crawl out of there if you have to! Usually lift attendants are on top of these situations and will help drag someone out of the way to avoid collisions. They will also stop the chair, if needed.

TROUBLESHOOTING

PROBLEM: Fear of falling on a steep unloading ramp.

SOLUTION:
The steeper the ramp, the greater the tendency for new riders to lean back in fear. Leaning back ensures that you will slide down the ramp on your backside. Don't fight the ramp. Ride it out with a flat board and a centered stance. Slow down to a stop with a heel- or toe-turn when you have more room and less incline.

5

6

7

❄ SURFACE LIFTS ❄

T-bars, platters and rope tows are not recommended for beginning riders. As you gain confidence and board-handling skills, you may find some cherished terrain that can only be accessed by a surface lift. In this case, you will have to master them.

Watch other riders boarding and note the amount of force in the initial tug. Stay as relaxed as possible and let the device TOW you. Don't sit down. Lean back against the tow and keep your board out in front of your body. Relax your knees to absorb bumps and irregularities in the lift track. You may have to use your edges to fight the wind or a slant in the lift track. Be ready for anything!

If you lose your balance, step off and push with your free leg and place it back on the board. Center yourself and bend your knees to regain balance. If you fall, let go of the tow and get out of the lift track so you don't cause others behind you to fall.

Don't use extra energy hanging on for dear life. Instead, think about hiking this same hill carrying your snowboard. Relax and let yourself move with the tow.

CHAPTER FOUR

Brakes and steering

Just off the chairlift, you look down your first hill.

Hopefully, you will be looking down a well-groomed

green (beginner) slope. If you're extra lucky, this

slope will have a uniform fall line and not too many

flat areas. After a few trips down this hill, you will

laugh at how steep it first looked!

The beauty of learning to snowboard is that it may slap you in the face with a bit of trepidation (or even snow) at first, but the basic control skills are so easy to grasp and the new movements feel so smooth so soon, that never-evers become lifetime enthusiasts very quickly.

FASTENING YOUR BACK FOOT AND STANDING UP

You have already made it through the most difficult part of the lesson: skating uphill and turning with the back foot free. Now comes the fun part. It's all downhill from here!

Find a spot at or near the edge of the hill to strap in your back foot. If you strap in too far away from the incline, you may have to unstrap and skate. Those with step-ins can still engage the back binding while sitting on a slight incline. It's better to have some initial incline, because it is easier to stand up and immediately adjust the balance.

Standing up on heel edge in a flat area is a difficult task for beginners. The angle of the hill will actually helps you stand up to feel the heel edge immediately.

2. To stand up get your body as close to the snowboard as possible.
3. As you stand up, commit your center of balance to a position directly over the heel edge.
4. As soon as you are standing up, begin sideslipping downhill to adjust your balance.

1. When you sit down to strap in your back foot ensure you are in a visible place away from jumps, hills or high-traffic areas

TESTING YOUR GAS PEDAL

One of the first skills you will learn as a new rider is "sideslipping". Sideslipping is learning to control the edge angle of a snowboard, perpendicular to the fall line, to enable the novice rider to slow down, side-slip an entire steep or dangerous run, or stop, if necessary. Slipping gives the new rider instant brakes and a gas pedal.

It doesn't really matter which edge you start out learning to slip on, heel or toe, because you will learn both. Many people have a hard time standing up on their heel side (**1**). If there is too much girth restricting you from crouching down to strap in, it will be difficult to get your center of gravity over the snowboard.

Usually, problems are due to a lack of commitment to standing up and taking control. You may be apprehensive about relinquishing complete control over gravity to the edge of a snowboard.

Until you trust enough to put your center of mass over the uphill edge, every attempt to stand up results in sitting back down. The first two rules of snowboarding come

into play: Keep Your Booty Over the Board and Trust Your Edges. A helping hand from an instructor will help you feel the quick movement of standing up on heel side without worrying about falling. There are subtle sliding adjustments that must take place when you first stand up (**2**), and holding on to a stable platform lets you to focus on what the body is doing without fear distracting you.

Still, some riders just cannot master the skill of standing up from the heel side on the first lesson. They can learn from their toe side first, and learn the heel side after a few of the concepts of how the center of mass relates to edge control have sunken in—along with a few bruises.

As we noted when learning to glide to a heel turn, most of us will have a preference for learning heel side first. This is especially true when learning slipping skills, because to travel downhill on the toe edge means to face uphill while sliding backward. This is not an easy concept for the mind to embrace right away.

Again, a helping hand is invaluable (**3**). Some can stand right up on their heel edge and start sliding downhill with perfect posture and control, and then there's the rest of us.

3

For some, it helps to have some support when first testing the gas and brakes of a snowboard. With balance assured, you can focus on how subtle movements in the ankles affect the amount of edge against the snow, which affects the speed that you travel.

THIRD RULE OF SNOWBOARDING: KEEP THE BOARD MOVING

Anytime the board is stationary, even on a flat surface, it is unstable. This is because both feet are attached to the same plane of balance. As humans, and skiers, we use both legs independently to adjust our balance when standing still, but when standing still on a snowboard, the only option is to sit down to stabilize the body.

So, if you want to maintain your balance when standing up on a board, keep it sliding at all times. As soon as you stand up, start sliding downhill to stabilize your balance.

HEEL SIDESLIPPING

Sideslipping is a chance to test the gas pedal and brakes of your snowboard by increasing or decreasing the edge angle of the board. You will be slipping directly down the fall line and keeping the board as perpendicular to it as possible (sideways to the hill).

fall line

uphill edge   edge angle   downhill edge

Keep your knees bent and your posture tall, while looking downhill, ahead of your board. Maintain your center of gravity over the heel edge, lean your calves against the highback, and feel the heel edge scraping snow downhill. Keep the board slightly out in front and experiment with slipping speeds by lifting your toes up to slow down and stop, and letting your toes drop to increase speed.

If your weight is not evenly distributed on both feet, the board will start to travel diagonally or even downhill. Keep the pressure equal on both heels and the board as sideways (perpendicular) to the fall line as possible.

When you get the feel of heel slipping, you have conquered a tall mountain in the quest for snowboard control. No matter how steep a hill you find yourself on, you can side-slip down safely. There is no longer any excuse to be flying downhill out of control with your eyes bugged out of your head. Keep your cool. Bring the board sideways, slide to a stop and gently sit down.

1. This rider is sideslipping with a low edge angle and, consequently, will slide downhill quickly.

❖ AVOIDING BODY SLAMS ❖

Body slams are caused by catching a downhill edge (see diagram opposite page). They just plain hurt. They even hurt to watch! The best way to avoid catching a downhill edge is to be absolutely committed to one edge or the other—heel or toe. On a steep slope, this is easy: There is more distance between the downhill edge and the snow.

But beware of level areas, "the flats!" For beginners, flat areas are much more hazardous than steep ones! If you get lazy and allow the downhill edge to come close to the snow, it could catch, sending your mass immediately to the center of the earth. BOOOOOM. Ouch. That's why they call them body slams—think pro wrestling.

Avoiding body slams is extremely important because these are the falls that really beat you up. Anytime the slope mellows out (becomes less steep), be aware of the downhill edge danger.

As the terrain becomes gentler, you will have to point the board more downhill, easing up to use less edge and maintain some speed.

Bending your knees and staying centered over the uphill edge will lessen the chances of catching a downhill edge by making it easier to keep the downhill edge up and away from the snow.

2. As she begins adjusting her board to a higher edge angle, the rider will start to slow down.

3. With a high edge angle, the board will come to a stop, but it will be difficult to balance upright while stationary.

TOE SIDESLIPPING

On toe sideslips, you will be slipping downhill while looking uphill. While first learning toe slips, it is nice to have some human support for confidence and balance, and to be your downhill eyes. Catching a downhill edge while toe sideslipping is twice as jarring as when heel sideslipping. Body slams from the toe side have even more force than from the heels, so keep the heel edge away from the snow.

Concentrate on feeling the toe edge and experiment with edge angles, just as you did with the heel sideslip (*see pages 52–53*). Increase the edge angle by tilting the board up and pressing your knees into the hill, and you will slow down and stop. Decrease the edge angle by letting your heels drop and the board will slide backward. Keep your center of gravity directly over the toe edge and your feet and board downhill of the rest of your body. Stand up tall and look straight ahead.

1

fall line

downhill edge   edge angle   uphill edge

The good thing about toe sideslipping, is that it is much easier to stand up from the toe edge. Just engage the toe edge (**a**), walk your hands up to the board (**b**) and stand up (**c**).

a

b

c

1. Letting the heels drop frees the board to slide downhill on the toe edge. Don't let that heel edge drop too far down to the body slam danger zone!

2. Slow down by bending the knees and pressing the toes into the slope more.

3. A high edge angle will stop you.

FALLING LEAF

Think of the way an autumn leaf falls to the ground. It doesn't drop straight like a rock; it sails the air currents. The thin, dry leaf glides side to side when each tip of the leaf dips toward the earth. A snowboard traverses (or moves diagonally across) the slope in much the same pattern, except that you are in control of its path, (unlike the leaf, which goes wherever the wind takes it).

As you may have discovered while experimenting with heel and toe slips (*pages 52–55*), when either tip of the board started to dip downhill, the board traveled sideways. You became aware that your weight was unevenly distributed and had to adjust back to slipping straight down the fall line. By equaling the pressure on both toes or both heels, you could bring the board sideways and even come to a complete stop.

Now, the board will dip on purpose, and travel across the hill in a diagonal line. This will be the first taste of speed: speed that you are in control of. Anytime you gain too much speed or a tree jumps out in front of you, bring the board sideways, sharply press in the heels or toes and scrape to a "hockey stop." This is a quick, noisy, stop that will come in very handy (*see opposite page*).

HOCKEY STOP

As you near the end of your traverse, slow down by putting more pressure on the back heel. When you are almost at a stop, let the back leg slide downhill and become the front leg. Switch your gaze to look in the opposite direction and traverse on your heel edge, riding fakie. You are already pulling off a freestyle trick!

1. Sometimes counter-rotating your upper body can be a useful skill if you need to stop quickly.

2. If another rider/skier or obstacle suddenly appears, press the back edges in firmly and the board will scrape sideways to an abrupt stop.

3. This works just as well on the toe side. Knowing that you can stop, no matter how fast you are traveling, will help you feel more confident as your speed increases.

THE WARRIOR STANCE

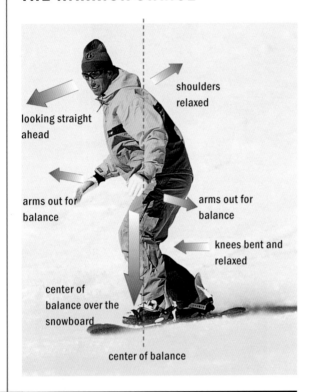

looking straight ahead

shoulders relaxed

arms out for balance

arms out for balance

knees bent and relaxed

center of balance over the snowboard

center of balance

PRO TIP

FOLLOW YOUR MIND

Karen Elliott
AASI Certified Level II
Instructor for Winter Park Rider
Improvement Center, Colorado

"If you set your mind to something, you can make it happen. Show your mind where you are going, and your body will follow. Looking at your board usually puts you on the ground with it, because looking only at the ground tends to make you bend at the waist, which throws you off balance. If you look down, all you see is the white ground, and your mind can't tell where it is. However if you can see the ground *and* the trees and the sky, you know exactly where you stand.

Where you look is where you go. Sometimes where you are looking is not where you want to end up. You don't want to become one with the trees and other riders and skiers, so when riding on congested slopes, try to concentrate on the spaces between the objects. Look ahead and anticipate the path you want to take."

TROUBLESHOOTING

PROBLEM: Leaning back on heelside traverse

SOLUTION: The normal human reaction to speed is to lean back, but as you learned while practicing turns with the back binding out (p. 38-41), putting the weight on your back leg cuts off the steering mechanism of the board, and makes you go even faster. Keeping your weight evenly distributed on both legs frees your back leg to pivot the board.

The best way to stand on the board while it is moving is the Warrior Stance. Think of yourself as an invincible gladiator (or Star Wars hero, whatever works) and your snowboard as your sword. Always be in the ready position: arms out for balance, knees bent, shoulders relaxed, looking ahead. What kind of warrior can fight effectively while scared stiff, bent over and looking at the ground?

The Warrior Stance is like the "ready" stance of any sport. If a line was drawn from the top of your head to the very center of your board, it would travel through your center of balance.

Your lower torso needs to be centered directly over the middle of the board, not flapping in the breeze behind you. When you bend in the waist, your center of balance is so far away from the edge you are trying to balance on, that you must straighten your knees to keep from falling over. When your legs are stiff, adjusting the edge angle of the board uses twice as much energy, which causes cramps in the calf muscles. But when the knees are bent, the ankles can easily make the needed balance adjustments.

Look ahead in the direction that you are traveling, and use the leading arm to point in that direction.

KEEP THE UPPER BODY STILL

It may seem that swinging the arms around will help the board turn, but this just wastes energy. When practicing garlands, you executed turns using only small movements of the lower body. Use only your hips, knees, ankles and toes to control the board.

If you are having a hard time getting the tail of the board around, then you are probably leaning back. Keep your weight centered over the board and your gaze and your mindset DOWNHILL. The tail of the board will slide around easily if you are not leaning on it. At any moment, you can chicken out of a turn and return to the same edge and even hockey stop (*see p. 57*), if needed.

If you are experiencing mental resistance, stop (in a safe place) and sit down on the snow. Watch other riders or close your eyes and imagine yourself confidently linking turn after perfect turn. Take your time, and analyze how each turn will look. Now, stand up and go for it.

Above: By using his arms to wind up for the turn, this rider's alignment is now off center.

Left: Instead of forcing the turns by swinging your arms around, save energy and use subtle pressure from your toes and heels to guide the board. This allows you to keep your gaze in the direction you are headed and work *with* the forces of gravity instead of *against* them.

TROUBLESHOOTING

PROBLEM: Straight legs, leaning back

SOLUTION: The rider has less leverage and less range of motion. It takes twice as much energy to lift the toes and press against the snow with the toe edge. With bent knees the rider engages all the leg muscles against gravity instead of overusing the calf muscles.

PROBLEM: Rider leaning back, front leg straight

SOLUTION: This rider's apprehension shows in her posture. When the front leg is straight and the back leg is bent, the rider's center of balance is too far back. The back leg will not turn very easily if all the weight is on it. Bending both knees equally will bring her center of balance back over the center of the board.

PROBLEM: Bending at the waist

SOLUTION: This rider is demonstrating "stinky riding." Many beginners bend at the waist and reach for the snow, thinking that by being closer to the snow, the fall will have less impact. This takes the center of balance away from the edge that is in contact with the snow, the toe edge. This makes his toe edge much less effective.

If you reach for the snow, that's where you'll end up. If you think about falling, you will. Stand up tall and use your knees and ankles as shock absorbers. Your waist can't do that job very effectively.

USING YOUR BOARD TO TRAVEL IN NEW WAYS

1 **2** **3**

SCOOTCHING Sometimes all you need to move is a few feet, but you don't want to unstrap and skate. You could hop (lots of energy) or you could scootch, a fore/aft rocking movement that moves the board forward first and the body catches up. Scootching does not work going uphill.

1. Slide the board out in front of you, pointing in the direction of travel.
2. Unweight the board with a subtle hop forward.
3. Bring your center of balance back over the board, a few feet ahead of where you were.

INCHWORMING If you need to move up a steeper hill without unstrapping, an inchworming movement will do for short distances. Just hop like a frog: arms first, then legs catch up, using the toe edge and hands as anchors. For longer distances, inchworming is too exhausting. It is better to take off the board and walk uphill.

PLAYING WITH THE TURN

With every turn linked, you will become more confident and less hesitant. You can take your mind off surviving each turn and start to play with gravity and your edges. As your confidence soars, your turns will become more rounded and smooth. Instead of jerking the board around frantically, you know the turn will happen, so you relax and use much less energy. Now it is time to experiment with gravity, snow and the sidecut of your board.

Try doing small-radius turns or big wide turns and hum a song to match your turns. Turn when the beat says instead of waiting until you are ready to turn. Try turns near both sides of the trail, and try bank turns off small moguls and inclines.

Being almost airborne as the turn occurs eases the rotation of the board. Rise up (less knee bend) before you

PRO TIP

CONTROLLING SPEED
Dena Melinn
Pro Boardercross Competitor

"Many factors come into play when you try to control your speed on a snowboard. Always be looking ahead so you can see changes in the terrain and be prepared.

To help with your control, keep your knees bent and stay centered over your board (ready position), so that you can react and adjust the board quickly and efficiently. Sharp edges ensure that you will have a dependable edge when it's time to stop or slow down.

Many people think speed is about pointing their board straight down the hill. They will go fast but with little control. It is safer to make wide-radius turns (carving is best) and to cruise at a comfortable speed. In time, we all get faster."

commit. Finish the curved turn by sinking your weight into the new edge. Bend the knees to absorb the centrifugal force of the turn. You will find that this up and down motion works to unweight you before the turn.

Try doing small jumps on flatter terrain. Start out when you are pointing the board downhill with no edge engaged and move up to small jumps while traversing. In short, play—focusing on sensations while you experiment with a new toy and the natural forces of gravity. Forget the grocery list and hassles at work. Pay attention to your body and your snowboarding, and your confidence will grow by leaps and bounds.

All good sport is about play—the process by which we allow ourselves to experiment and make mistakes, all with the aim of getting better.

PRO TIP

TEASING THE FALL LINE
Jeff "the Fog" Smith
Certified level III AASI
snowboard instructor

"Instead of making the same old boring turn, try using terrain creatively, making turns of varying sizes and shapes and at different speeds. If there is a steep pitch that intimidates you, tease the fall line, then chicken out, making your way across the slope. Your "chicken turns" should look like a series of half-turns. The angle of your "chicken turns" should be gentle at first, and as your confidence increases, let the tip of the board seek progressively steeper descents.

Once you've mastered the "chicken turn," try adding more edge, speed and shape. This exercise helps develop good foot steering, edging and pressure skills, and will give you more options when you encounter terrain that you perceive as over your ability level."

SLOPE SURVIVAL

As soon as you begin to link turns, you will become part of the flow of downhill traffic. This is both exhilarating and hazardous. Soon, carving toe and heel turns will become a spontaneous dance with the mountain, but at first, it will take intense concentration to do it right, and you might suffer from "tunnel vision."

Unlike skiers, snowboarders have a "blind side" on the heel turn, when their back is turned away from downhill traffic. The best solution is to frequently check uphill, over your back shoulder so you know where the traffic around you is headed. The downhill skier or rider has the right-of-way, but many collisions can be prevented by checking uphill, especially in crowded areas and where trails merge.

Even if you are resting, you must be aware of traffic. Skiers can rest standing up, but riders usually sit down, and this makes them less visible to uphill traffic. Never rest under a knoll or "hit." Choose a more visible place to sit down.

TROUBLESHOOTING CATWALKS

PROBLEM: Catwalks are narrow, groomed areas designed to transport riders and skiers across a mountain. They can be unnerving as there is limited real estate on which to turn and not much pitch to help. If a rider has to stop, it may mean unstrapping and skating to get going again. Snowboarders don't want to stop and lose downhill momentum, and the snowboard's scritching noise from checking speed can alarm others. Many catwalks have a slanted fall line, requiring riders to rely on one edge over the other, causing cramps in the calves.

SOLUTIONS: Stay as uphill as possible and close to the sides of the catwalk. (At least trees don't move.) Make small turns to check your speed and communicate with downhill traffic by (gently) announcing your intentions. For skiers, let them know you are coming on the right or on the left. For other riders, indicate that you will be passing them on the heel or toe side. Be polite. Thank others for letting you pass. Smiling is free and painless.

Always leave yourself an "out": enough room to yank the board around to a hockey stop. People are in their own little worlds and do unpredictable (and yes, stupid) things on the slope, just as they do behind the wheel. So forgive easily and ride friendly. This is recreation, not war.

PRO TIP

COPING WITH THE FLATS

Wayne Snyder PSIA level II certified snowboard instructor, Loveland Ski Area, Colorado

"On steeper terrain, there is more room between the downhill edge and the slope (more edge angle), but in the flats, novice riders sometimes catch a downhill edge. Keep the weight on the front foot to keep the board pointing down the fall line, and keep your center of mass over the edge you're on. If you know the run well, you know when to point the board downhill and not check your speed, so you don't get stuck in the flats.

On slopes that slant to one side and are relatively flat, you will need to traverse to stay uphill. Keep more weight on the front foot. Sticking to one edge may be painful but necessary. If you get too far downhill on a slanted flat slope, you may need to take one binding out and 'stair-step' uphill or take both feet out of the bindings and walk up carrying the board."

CHAPTER SIX

Harnessing the power of the turn

BORN TO CARVE

A snowboard is born to carve. If pressure is applied equally from both feet into the edge that is in contact with the snow, the snowboard will naturally draw a circle with that edge.

Most boards have sidecuts that produce a medium-size circle radius of six to eight yards (8–9m), allowing for an effortless turn with maximum stability. Deeper sidecuts produce tighter, quicker turns but will be less stable than boards with a larger sidecut, which produces wider, slower turns.

Choosing the right amount of sidecut will always be a game of compromise. The deeper the sidecut, the less versatile the snowboard. You can opt for an all-mountain do-everything board, or have a "quiver" of specialized snowboards designed for specific uses, such as a GS board and a slalom board. The sidecut of the GS board produces long, wide turns that can withstand speed. The deeper sidecut of the slalom board produces tighter, quicker turns. Neither would be the board of choice for a deep powder day or a session in the halfpipe.

CARVING BASICS

Find a well groomed slope to first practice carving, and examine the tracks you leave behind. Are they clean, deep ruts or smeared? Listen. Is your edge slicing or scraping?

fall line

1   **2**   **3**

To begin on your lifetime quest to perfect the carve, we have to go back to basics again. Remember that first day when you were traversing the bunny hill, having your first blast of speed on a snowboard?

Start on a mellow green (beginner) or blue (intermediate) slope that is well groomed and not icy. Keeping your weight as centered as possible, practice toe and heel traverses while trying to leave a distinct rut in the snow (**1**). If the track you cut is wide and smeared, bend your knees into the hill more and lift your toes or heels more by making small adjustments with your ankles (**2**). This increases the edge angle of your board and puts the edge against the snow instead of the whole blade.

A high edge angle supports more weight by utilizing the design of the snowboard. This allows the board to do most of the work to turn instead of your muscles. Try to make the tail edge of your board pass through the exact same rut that the nose edge started, keeping your weight

evenly distributed between both feet. You want the pressure on the "sweet spot" of the sidecut—between the front and back bindings. When you are able to leave a decent rut on both heel and toe sides, point the board more downhill and practice carving garlands on heel and toe sides (**3**).

If you're lucky, the area where you are practicing carving has a groomed trail under the path of the chairlift. From up there, you will have a helicopter view of your successful and not-so-successful carves. The feedback of each turn is written in the snow.

As you perfect your garlands, play "chicken" by pointing the board more downhill, carving a more complete circle by switching edges at a 2 or 3 o'clock position instead of a 4 or 5 o'clock position. If you gain too much speed on the downhill, slow down by maintaining the circle and starting uphill. This is your "emergency brake" and is invaluable to you as a tool to increase your confidence.

4   **5**   **6**

When you first start to link carved turns, you will find that it is easier to complete the turn if the forces of gravity are suspended for a moment. Try unweighting at the start of your uphill momentum and completing the turn while there is minimal pressure on the snowboard (**4**). Then sink into a deep knee bend and a high edge angle as you complete the turn (**5**). You will find this up and down motion (extension and flexion of the knees and ankles) very energy-efficient.

There are many factors that interact to define the carve that you attempt. More speed will require a higher edge angle and icy slope conditions will add more challenge to holding that edge against the forces of gravity. The more you lean towards the snow on your uphill edge, the higher the edge angle that you can produce (**6**). There is a breaking point, but it is amazing how far you can actually lean into the hill before the edge will lose its grip.

Starting the turn early will help you reduce skidding by dissipating the centrifugal force throughout the turn.

ANGULATION

By positioning your body just
so, you can increase the range
of inclination without sliding
or skidding. Angulation is
using your knees, ankles and
hips to increase the edge angle
while increasing the stability of
the turn. Angulation allows
you to keep your center of
balance over the board edge by
driving your hips and knees
toward the snow and into the
turn (**1**). By using your knee
and ankle joints to increase the
edge angle (**2**), you will be in a
better position to react (slow

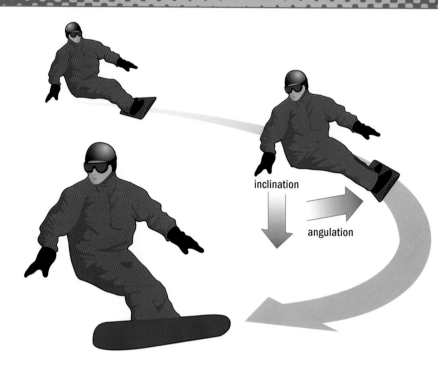

inclination

angulation

1

2

down, stop, turn quickly, or jump over an obstacle) than if you were in a laid-out position on the carve. It's a delicate balance between the amount of inclination set against the amount of angulation you need to carve an efficient turn. As you perfect the carve, you will be astonished at how far you can push the limits of gravity and still come out of a fast turn on your feet (**3**).

Nobody has to tell you that you are not carving well. Your tracks tell one side of the story and your decibel level the other. Your ears will alert you immediately when you are not carving efficiently. That scritching noise is so irritating, that once you are aware of it and know how to fix the squeak, you will focus on your carving skills in the name of noise prevention. Your fellow snowboarders and skiers will thank you.

3

PRO TIP

CARVING 101
Meade Parks Veteran Enduro competitor and 2002 Giant Slalom champion.

"Carving a complete turn is a combination of feel and technique. You have to be able to feel the entire edge of the board and know when to put pressure on certain parts of the edge. Heelside carves always seem to be easier in the beginning, so start with a heelside cut.

The idea is to lower your body before the carve so you can extend throughout the turn as needed. Pushing your heels pressures that edge. You want to push until you are at the apex of the turn, then start to let up a little to maintain a carve, not skid out or hook. This will allow you to finish the heelside turn.

Key points to a complete carve:
1. Always maintain a posture that is downhill to the fall line and look way ahead and at where you want to turn.
2. Pretend to be reaching for your upside edge as you are carving (the edge not on the snow) this will help keep your arms and shoulders level.
3. Use your back leg as a lever and drive it out or in as needed to maintain your edge contact with the snow.
4. There is very rarely a perfect carve from start to finish, so don't get frustrated. Just keep trying to make what feels like a perfect carve."

CHAPTER SEVEN
Freestyle

When most people think of snowboarding, they think of freestyle. It's the flashy, "show-time" side of riding that appears everywhere from snowboard magazine covers to soft drink commercials. Advertisers love to equate their product with the daring, radical, with-it image of freestyle snowboarding tricks and the crazy dudes who pull them off.

It's no wonder that so many new riders want to huck themselves huge before even learning to turn and stop. They've seen it on TV and that's what snowboarding means to them. But if you've come this far in your snowboarding education then you have mastered the basics and realize that snowboarding is so much more than phat air, spins and tweaking it out.

But chances are, getting airborne has been in the back of your mind since you even thought about strapping on a snowboard. As you were patiently working on your control and balance, you had a few tastes of freestyle moves to come: riding fakie on your first traverses, to (perhaps) unintentional air off small bumps or knolls. Now it's time to learn to fly and spin. Fasten your seatbelts and get ready for some real fun!

LANDING SAFELY

Anything goes if you don't care about the landing, but if you want to jump and land on your feet without injury, you must go back to the basic rules of riding: Keep your Booty over the Board and Bend your Knees.

You won't last long jumping (or doing anything!) on a snowboard with straight legs. To preserve your precious knees, you must land gently and absorb the impact of the jump by bending in the knees and ankles. You can decrease the amount of stress on your whole body by sinking into the landing instead of resisting it. If you lock your knees and stiffen up, you are bound to cartwheel. It's better to fold up and slide to a stop with less chance of injury.

Another knee-saver: Make sure any jump you are attempting has at least as steep a landing as the take-off. Flat landings can rip your knee ligaments. Why chance it? If it's a big jump and the landing is not visible, scout it out first and take it on the next run.

Enthusiasm and one-upmanship can sometimes blind us to common sense. We're all guilty of this at one time or another, but when you're attached to a snowboard and launching yourself into the atmosphere, there is more at stake. Use your head.

START SMALL

In the flats, you can change directions while attached to the board with a 180° jump. Twist the upper body first then jump and bring the lower body around.

1

2

There's a good chance that you have already experienced "getting air." You have probably hopped short distances on flat areas to avoid unstrapping and strapping in again, or you may have jumped up and down to shake snow off the board.

The flats are a perfect place to practice first jumps. Since there is absolutely no slope or speed to deal with, you are forced to jump off a flat board and land on a flat board.

Take this concept with you on the hill and you will love jumping from your first attempt.

When you feel confident jumping up and down in place (**1–3**), bring your knees (and snowboard) up more or try a half-turn (180) by first twisting the upper body in the opposite direction that you want to spin. Then swing the upper body while jumping up. The lower body follows and completes the 180° rotation (**4–5**).

ACTIVE AIR

The amount of extension and flexion in your knees and ankles can greatly influence the amount of air you achieve. With active air, you start low and spring off the height of the jump to get higher and enjoy more air time.

A jump that starts off right will continue that way, but if you begin unbalanced or on edge, your situation will not improve as you fly through the air. The take-off is very important, so relax and think smooth and flat. Once committed to the jump and within ten yards (10m) of take off, don't check your speed. Just go for it. Chickening out at the last minute is why many riders get hurt while jumping.

Like your first turns, your mind is not going to like the idea of pointing the board downhill and picking up speed.

OLLIES

An ollie is a fantastic skill to use in all kinds of situations. It allows you to get bigger air out of a jump, but instead of using only your legs for power, the ollie uses the energy of the board's camber (*see page 125*).

When you lift the nose of the board, you spring off the tail, lifting the rear foot and the entire board into the air. If you were to do this movement on the ground with no snowboard attached, it would look and feel like a side jump— front foot up and over, followed by the back foot springing up and joining the front foot.

Ollies can be useful if you are traveling fast and don't want a jump to send you flying into a blind landing. Ollies can also be used to jump over obstacles like rocks, branches, streams etc. when there is no kicker (*see Glossary, page 8*).

1

2

But the safest way to go is to let gravity win until the jump is completed, then use your edges to slow down. While airborne, your board is easy to move around. Scoot it under your body and center yourself before the landing, keeping your gaze straight ahead and looking to where you will land. You can tell when a rider is not centered inflight. "Rolling down the windows" or using the arms for wings are good indications that the jump started off-balance.

When you are just about to land, extend your legs and sink into the downward slope with your knees and ankles soft (see right), and then check your speed.

3   **4**

1. The instant before becoming airborne, shift your weight to your back foot.
2. Spring off the tail of the board, using the board's camber to spring you higher and further.
3. Keep the board centered underneath you and look ahead to the landing.
4. Use your knees, ankles and hips to absorb the impact of the landing. Practice doing ollies without a jump by leaping over shadows, twigs and bumps.

GRABS

Grabs look and feel cool, but most important, they keep you compressed and at one with your board while flying. Start with the most basic of grabs, the indy, grabbing the toeside edge with your trailing hand between your feet.

It is more efficient to bring your legs and board up to your hand rather than bending over to reach for the board. Bending at the waist forces the entire body out of balance by moving your center of balance to one side and starting forward momentum toward the toeside, almost ensuring a crash landing.

Try grabbing the tail, the nose, and the heel edge. Grab with both hands at once or two separate grabs in the same air. There is no end to the combinations and variations. Create your own signature grab!

1. Start the jump with a solid take-off and a centered stance over your flat board. Look in the direction you will be landing.
2. Bring the board up to your hand instead of bending over to reach it. (Flexibility and strong core muscles come in handy!)
3. A mute grab, boned out. (The back hand grabs between the feet on the toe edge; the legs are straight.)

TERRAIN PARKS

Terrain parks were originally designed for freestyle riders but have become the newest hangout of freeskiers and shorty-skiers. This new style of ski borrowed its twin-tip design from freestyle snowboards, allowing a skier to go off jumps fakie, land fakie, or do almost anything a snowboarder can do.

Terrain parks have done much to mend the rifts between snowboarders and skiers and have given everyone a safe place to go big. The best terrain parks are maintained religiously by a dedicated mountain resort and are packed with rail slides, green, blue, black and double-black jumps with steep landings, berms, snakes, halfpipes and quarterpipes.

Resorts have tried to outdo each other with imaginative and challenging features and many provide benches, garbage cans, warm-up yurts (tents), tools, music and water- and snack-vending machines. Many "park rats" will never leave the park all day, hiking the halfpipe and their favorite hits with their riding buddies.

PRO TIP

TERRAIN PARK ETIQUETTE
Christy Olin
USASA national all-around champion—boardercross, halfpipe, slopestyle, GS, and Slalom

"Terrain parks can appear to be intimidating, but there is some order in the chaos and certain understood rules which make the experience more relaxing, safe, and fun for everyone.

IN THE PARK

BE AWARE
Always be extremely conscious of the terrain and those around you. Avoid resting, watching or riding in any landing or take-off areas.

BECOME FAMILIAR
Before launching off any jumps, take at least one run through the park to become familiar with the hits. Watch other riders and note how much speed they use for each jump.

BE PATIENT
When you are ready to attack the park, you may have to wait in line at each jump to allow each rider enough time to move safely out of the way. Make sure to see the previous jumper move out of the way before proceeding. If you cannot see the landing, have a friend or ski patrol "spot" or watch the landing for you.

USE SPEED
This is a little tricky at first, but will come with practice and a few bruises. Try to remember the speed that others used to hit the jumps and try to mimic them as closely as possible. Most jumps have a certain distance to clear and a set area on which to land. Missing the landing could result in injury or embarrassment.

MOVE!
After you clear a jump, get out of the way! If you wreck, slide, crawl or drag yourself to a safe area out of the way of oncoming riders.

IN THE PIPE

LINES
Like the park, you may encounter lines at the halfpipe. Those in the right line alternate with those in the left line. Some may want a toeside or heelside hit first; some are goofy, some regular. If the pipe is crowded, yell "dropping!" when entering, which cuts down on confusion.

TIMING
The person in front of you might be slower, and if you catch up, you'll have to slow down. Pay attention to the speed and ability of the rider ahead of you when they enter the pipe. Don't be rude—everyone starts out as a newbie.

FALLING
If you do fall, which happens to everybody, get up as soon as possible and exit the pipe so you won't get hurt. Never go straight down the pipe when people are in it."

RAILS

Rail slides, like many tricks in freestyle riding, have their roots in skateboarding. The original rail slides were down stairwell railings, but resorts are installing them in terrain parks: short, tall and even curved. Short, wide rails are best for learning. Most have a slight kicker to get you up onto the rail. A slide with the length of the board in line with the rail is called a 50/50 because the board is balanced on the arches, equally between heels and toes.

If you feel your board start to drift toward your heels or toes, it's best not to fight it. If you try too hard to hold onto the slide, you could land on the rail. (Ouch!) Just try to go further next time. When you are sliding with ease, add an air with a grab or twist as you dismount the rail.

1. Start out with the most basic rail slide, a 50/50, with your board pointing straight ahead.
2. If you aren't perfectly centered you can jump off the rail and continue riding downhill.
3. It's better to concede and jump off than to endure a painful fall on to the rail.

HALFPIPE

The halfpipe is another skateboard-inspired terrain park feature that has become so popular, a grooming machine— the Pipe Dragon—has been invented just to shape and maintain it. The Pipe Dragon has a transitionally shaped cutting arm which is towed behind a snowcat.

Most halfpipes are about 5 yards (3–4m) deep and about 75 yards (100m) long. The newer Superpipe Dragons can produce "Superpipes" that have 30 percent increases over standard measurements.

The frontside wall is the one that you will face on your toe edge. For regular stance, the frontside wall will be the one on your right as you look down from the drop-in area. For goofy-footers, the frontside wall will be on the left.

The backside wall is the one where your back will be to the wall: the left wall for regulars, right wall for the goofies. Backside air is usually more difficult to master than frontside air.

DROPPING IN
Christine Sperber
Freestyle Coach, Burton
Snowboards, Summit County,
Colorado

"So, it's your first time in the halfpipe...relax. Everyone was a beginner once. Feel free to sit and watch for a while, but don't place yourself in the way of riders entering the pipe or hang out close enough to the lip to be in the way of riders launching tricks. Unplanned exits do happen. When you are ready to drop in, leave enough space between yourself and the rider ahead of you. (I use two hits as a good rule.) Raise a hand and call out "dropping" or "next."

All the best riders I have met are encouraging and supportive of new pipe riders, but the best time to try the pipe is not on a sunny afternoon, when it's full of ripping riders pushing each other to go bigger.

The most success I've had in teaching halfpipe is with a drill using the falling leaf (see page 56). Choose whatever edge you are most comfortable with and ride it back and forth across the pipe without turning. Pump the transition like you would a swing to generate more speed, but not too much. Know your limits! The goal is to get as many hits back and forth as you can. When you become comfortable on that edge, switch to the other. Don't try to turn until you are comfortable on both edges.

Think about the line your edge leaves in the snow on your way up the wall and aim for that line when you make your way back down. Don't jump or turn until all your forward momentum has stopped. Just remember: straight up; straight down; bend your knees; look where you are going. But you are a snowboarder now, which means you will most likely ignore my advice and just go for it anyway."

PRO TIP

SKILLS IN THE PIPE
Dave Miner
Certified level III AASI instructor,
Breckenridge, Colorado

Riding the pipe is basically doing heel and toe turns on a blue groomed slope that has walls on each side. It helps to be centered and have equal pressure on both feet. You should be able to do smooth, carved turns before even thinking about riding the halfpipe.

Here the rider is on her uphill edge, her center of mass (waist, hips, bellybutton) is right over the edge that's in contact with the snow . She is committed downhill and already looking ahead at the other wall (1–2). Many first-timers drop into the pipe leaning back in fear and they crash right away or they reach for the wall, which zaps their speed. They'll never get out of the pipe.

As the rider rotates in the air, her entire body is aligned with the longitudinal axis of the board (3–4). Her hips and her shoulders are rotating with the length of the board (5).

Demonstrating a backside air the rider waits for the height of her trick to rotate. With all that height, she has plenty of time for the grab (6). She brings the board up to her hand instead of reaching for it (7).

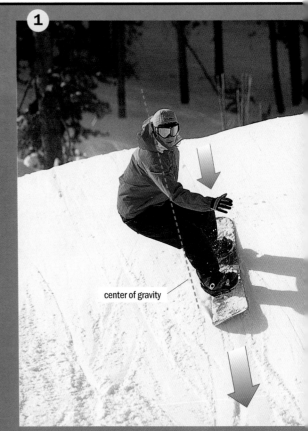

1

center of gravity

4

axis

5

axis

CHAPTER EIGHT

Riding the gnarly

Just because weather or snow conditions aren't perfect doesn't mean that it's not a good day to ride. It's *always* a good day to ride. Sure, we would rather have a warm, sunny day and new snow, groomed to buttery perfection, but usually we have to deal with reality. Instead of bumming out on what Mother Nature has to offer, view gnarly conditions as an opportunity to become a more versatile rider—one who can ride just about anything.

ICE OR HARDPACK

Depending on what part of the world your snow fell upon, icy conditions (or "hardpack"—a more pleasant-sounding description that mountain resorts prefer to use) could be an occasional or a daily challenge.

Some of the best competitive riders come from mountainous areas of the planet that have a more humid climate, and hence, firmer (icier) snow conditions. Since a lazy carving technique simply won't cut it on ice, these riders learn to use their edges very efficiently. Their refined carving skills help them achieve more speed out of the halfpipe and lose less time snaking around racing gates. So when nature offers you lemons (icy slopes), make lemon sorbet: Use ice to improve or measure your carving skills.

Starting with a well-tuned board is the best way to go into battle. Your edges need to be razor sharp (90 to 88 degrees) to grip the hardpack. As long-time alpine snowboard coach, Steve Stevenson says, "The only board that doesn't need to be tuned is one that just got tuned."

Snowboard shops carry "diamond stones," small personal tuning files of varying coarseness. These can be slipped into a pocket and used for touching up edges between runs. Riding tuned is riding safe.

TAKING CONTROL

For ice, the best equipment set-up is hard boots, plate bindings, and an alpine board. Hard boots, resembling ski boots, offer a better transfer of energy from the feet to the board. Alpine boards are made to hug ice at fast speeds, but are not designed to ride fakie or to spin as well as a freestyle or all-mountain board.

But most riders don't want (or can't afford) two sets of snowboarding equipment. Riding hardpack is possible with a freestyle set-up, but you will have to put in more effort. Stiffer, longer, all-mountain boards with maximum edge contact are preferred over short boards that are designed for spinning air maneuvers in the terrain park.

Tighten the laces of your boots and the straps on your bindings to gain the least amount of "swimming" of your foot in the boot. Heel anchors are like rubber heel cups that fit between the liner and outer layers of the boot and weave into the outer lacing. The tighter you pull the outer laces, the snugger the heel-fit. Sometimes, something as simple as a pair of small heel lifts can greatly reduce energy leaks in a freestyle boot.

Orthotics, or personal footbeds, also help fit by customizing the fit of the foot's sole with the bottom of the boot, and reducing pressure points when the boots and bindings are tightened.

PRO TIP

DIAL UP YOUR FORWARD LEAN
Lowell Hart
Director of the Keystone Snowboarding School, Keystone Resort, Colorado

"Does your board ever sketch out from underneath you on a hard heelside turn? Do you butt-check when the going gets steep, the snow is hard, or when landing a big air—especially on the scraped-off sections? If so, you may want to adjust a simple mechanism on the back of your binding. It can instantly lead to higher levels of performance on your snowboard.

Blowing out on the heel edge can be caused by shabby technique, by an overhanging boot and binding, or by a poorly tuned or too-soft board. However, one of the main reasons riders bail (fall) on the heel edge is that they have too little forward lean on their bindings. If you find yourself losing it on the heel edge—especially when the going gets steep or icy—check your binding's forward lean adjustment. Having the right amount of lean is often the difference between a high-speed sketch (having your board slide out from under you) and sticking the turn or landing cleanly. Adjusting the forward lean on your bindings can instantly turn you into a better rider. Here's how to check and adjust yours:

Locate the adjusting mechanism behind your highback. This simple mechanism connects to the highback and contracts the binding's heel cup. By lowering the mechanism, you can increase the amount of forward lean on your highback. If your highback stands straight up, reposition it (you may need a screwdriver to do this) so that your highback tilts toward your toe edge. Most pros are riding between 18 and 25 degrees forward lean; experiment until you find the amount of lean that's right for you.

Increasing the amount of forward lean will allow you to tilt the board on its heel edge using a small movement of the knee, rather than making a big movement of the butt. Making the movement with your knee allows you to tilt the board on its edge quicker while keeping your weight over the board. This allows you to ride steeps, bumps and ice more effectively. It also allows you to ride heelside with your knees bent, which is often the difference between sketching and standing, especially at higher speeds or when landing airs."

CHILL ON ICE

The first rule of ice is to *relax*. If you panic and freeze up, you will skid. If you bend your knees and go with the flow, you will be able to react to what's under your feet. Look ahead at what's coming up and avoid the middle sections of trails where traffic is highest. Patches right under the crest of a hill are notorious icy spots, because skiers and riders check their speed here. Avoid these areas and you will avoid much of the ice. Stick to the sides of the trail and pick a spot past the ice patch where snow has built up to turn. Instead of fighting the ice, choose your turns wisely.

Slow down, keeping your weight centered directly over the edge that is in control. Keep the pressure as equal as possible between the feet throughout the turn. The more pressure you have on your front or back foot, the more the board will skid. If you can't perform pure, carved turns, you will have trouble with ice. Take a carving lesson during a good snow day and learn how to get more efficiency and power out of each turn. It will improve all aspects of your riding.

PRO TIP

BALANCE ON ICE

Justin Goto

Alpine racer on USASA Junior World Team, Steamboat Springs, Colorado

"Ice is the hardest, most aggressive snow condition you can encounter on the hill. You would think that an aggressive riding style would be the key to overcoming this slippery nuisance, but actually, when you encounter ice your style of riding needs to be feather-light, with minimal weight transfers.

The key to handling ice is to acquire complete fore/aft and lateral balance over the edge that is in contact with the snow, by putting downward pressure on that edge and creating a stable platform."

THE STEEPS

Steepness is a relative term. What may seem death-defying to one rider could bore another. What may have seemed steep on your first week of snowboarding may seem like a kindergarten playground on your second week. Or the exact same steep trail could seem easy on a powder or slush day and impossible on an icy day. Regardless of what you consider a steep slope, the problems you faced when you first started linking turns will resurface on "the steeps." It all boils down to committing to the turn and trusting your edges to catch you.

Stay centered over the edge of your board and stand tall (remember the Warrior Stance, p. 58), with flexible knees and your arms out for balance. If it's really steep, deep or crusty, you may have to hop your turns around like a kangaroo.

Steep (not icy steep) is actually one of the easiest gnarly territories for intermediates to conquer. There is no way that you can catch a downhill edge. If you commit to the turn, it will happen. It's when you chicken out and lean back in fear that all the face plants and cartwheels occur. Keep your gaze and your mindset downhill!

Avoid icy *and* steep. If you skid out on a turn, you could slide the remainder of the run, unable to slow down or stop. (Very dangerous—not to mention embarrassing.)

THE BUMPS

Moguls, or "the bumps," are especially troublesome to beginner and intermediate riders. Even some riders who consider themselves advanced avoid the bumps like the plague because they can tame a rider's ego pretty quickly.

The best bump riders usually have a more downhill facing stance dialed into their bindings (Bob Garven has 39 degrees on the front foot and 3 degrees on the back foot in the bump sequence opposite), so they can face downhill with a quiet upper body while the lower body snakes around the moguls.

It helps to have lightning-quick reflexes and strong core muscles (back, stomach, trunk, yes—more sit-ups), and it doesn't hurt to have the ultimate confidence in your turning abilities. In short, beginner and intermediate riders may want to perfect their turns on groomed slopes before venturing into the "forest of no return."

To learn bumps the gentle way, practice bank turns (heel and toe) off occasional small bumps found on blue (intermediate) runs. Experiment by turning on top of the bump, on both sides, and in the trough between bumps.

Start out on soft bumps, preferably on a slush or powder day. Soft snow is more forgiving and will build your confidence in the moguls.

When you feel ready to do battle with the bumps, find a trail with round moguls and soft snow. Powder and slush (heavy, melted snow) conditions are perfect for learning bumps, because there is much more cushioning on falls and more room for error in the turns. Icy bump runs are pure torture. Don't even go there...

Riding bumps is extremely aerobic! Try linking a handful of turns, then sit down and rest (in a visible place). As you perfect your mogul skills, you will link more turns and rest less often. An aggressive, never-say-die attitude is essential to taking on moguls. Like riding the steeps, mastering bumps requires an all or-nothing downhill attitude.

PRO TIP

GETTING INTO THE BUMPS
Bob Garven
2001 USASA boardercross, slalom, and GS champion for men 40-49. Currently has a 14-year streak of riding at least 200 days a year.

"Think you're ready for the moguls? You should first be able to make small, fast turns. Try to find a run with small bumps on one side and a groomed surface on the other. Do small turns on the groomed area but right next to the bumps. Imagine turning like that in the bumps. Make a bank turn on one of the outside bumps, then go back to groomed surface. Practice this a few times. This is half of what mogul riding is all about.

Now go around the bump turn and do the bank turn on the other side of the next bump over, practicing these forays into the bumps next to the groomed area. You can pop out of the bumps if you get in trouble and gain control on the flat surface. Always keep your knees bent and use them as shock absorbers. Stay low and react to the surprises. Keep your upper body quiet and let the legs do most of the work.

If you can link two bank turns or more then you're mogul riding. Moguls are one of the hardest things to ride well on a snowboard, but don't let that stop you. They can be excellent fun. Look at mogul runs as natural terrain parks. Each bump can be used as a ramp to air."

RIDING THE BUMPS

While the rider's lower body snakes around the moguls, his upper body remains relatively calm. His gaze is downhill, his knees are soft and his shoulders rarely dip out of alignment.

POWDER

Riding powder is the ultimate snowboarding experience! Powder gives you the freedom to try steeper runs, since the deep snow holds you back. It cushions big air and makes even the most radical moves effortless. If you have dreamed it, you can do it—on a "pow" day.

Riding powder is a psychological cure-all. No matter how bad your life is going, a pow session will make it better. But this powerful natural high can also be addictive. Riders who are normally stable, patient and unselfish have been known to abandon their own mother or miss their own wedding for a pow day. (But if it were true love, they would be out in the freshies together, mutually blowing off the wedding.)

Your first experience with powder can be like your first kiss. You dream about how wonderful it will be, but when it presents itself, you don't know exactly what to do with it.

First experiment with patches of powder along the sides of groomed trails. Just straight-run it and get the feel of your snowboard floating through the snow. No matter how many times you experience powder, you will never get over the thrill of watching your board slice through it!

Bounce or "porpoise" the board up and down by increasing and decreasing the flex of the knees. Since you don't need to put as much pressure on your edges, your leg movements can be softer and more fluid. If you keep your weight centered over the middle of the board, the rest will magically fall into place. (That's a promise from the Powder Goddess.)

If you fall down and get stuck, get back on the groomed section of the trail and regain your speed. Maintaining speed is important in deep snow, especially when the trail is less steep. *Avoid anything deep that isn't steep!* If you don't have some groomed slope nearby, you could end up stuck, and expend enormous amounts of energy "swimming" out of there.

If it's a cold day, you may want some fresh wax. (See chapter 9 for advice on maintaining your board.) Nothing is more frustrating than slowing down in the flats because your base is sticking to the new snow.

You can literally choke on powder that is flying back in your face as you sail through it! Hence the phrase, "It was so deep, I had to use a snorkel!" When the powder is deep, there is nothing for the board's edge to bite into, so don't fight it. Go with the flow. These are the "epic" days you will tell your grandchildren about. It shouldn't take you long to fall in love with pow, maybe just a few turns.

I was going to tie up this section on powder with a good anecdote or tip, but it just started snowing, and all of a sudden, I gotta go...

FLAT LIGHT

Flat light or reduced visibility due to a blizzard can turn any experienced rider into a beginner again. We rely on vision so heavily that when we are robbed of it, we feel helpless. Sometimes flat light can cause queasiness, like a carnival ride, as the mind struggles to decipher which way is up and down.

During blizzard conditions avoid high alpine slopes that are above the tree line and wear goggles with low-light lenses. Stay in or near the trees, and use trees, trail signs, ropes and other people on the slopes to judge steepness and distance. Don't blindly follow someone, however, or you may find yourself following them straight to trouble. Ride safely and smartly, and learn to trust your instincts.

Work on developing other senses, like touch and hearing, when riding. When you are on an uncrowded green slope, try a few turns with your eyes closed (you can peek a little). Really feel the edge of your board on the snow and use your knees to absorb unexpected bumps. Listen carefully to the board slicing the snow and hear other riders and skiers before they get close to you. Then, when you find yourself in a low-light situation, remind yourself that you can do it with your eyes closed.

DEATH COOKIES AND CRUD

"Death cookies" are frozen chunks of snow hidden beneath new snow that can throw you off balance instantly. Slow down and put your board in "front-wheel drive." Keep your weight centered and ride the crud like moguls, using your knees to absorb the irregularities. Look ahead and try to avoid what you can, but when you do hit crud, think neutral. It is better to concede and move gently over a rough spot than to fight it.

SLUSH

Slush can be as fun as powder! While skiers are struggling through mounds of heavy, exhausting slush, snowboarders are cruising by like waterskiers at mach speed. The thicker the better, dude!

Slush is consistent and soft like powder, but more leg muscle and edge pressure are required. Slush makes it easier to control your speed and provides a soft landing for tricks. Spring snow can vary immensely in density depending on sun exposure. Shaded areas can harbor soft snow, but hitting a sunny spot can stop you dead and send you flying. Riding in shorts and a T-shirt on a warm day might seem like a good idea, but one good wipeout will change your mind. Wear appropriate clothing at all times.

TREES

Trees and pow go together like coffee and cream. But while powder slows you down and makes the turns effortless, riding the trees can be dangerous. Trees are not very forgiving, so a wrong move could be a painful one.

Experiment along the sides of the trail, ducking into the woods when you see a comfortable space between trees. Look into the woods when you are riding this close and imagine yourself turning in the spaces of powder between the trees.

When you are ready to venture in, pick a widely spaced glade with lots of "outs" available. Keep your gaze two or three trees ahead and look for the spaces, not at the trees. Dive into tighter trees when you acquire more confidence. Deep powder makes the turns effortless, but be sure to keep up your speed in the woods. Falling or stopping could mean "swimming" in chest-deep snow to upright yourself and get going again.

Helmets? That's a no-brainer! Mandatory! And—if you value your life—never, *never* ride off-limits.

OFF-PISTE

Off-piste is anywhere off the groomed run, but this term can vary in meaning throughout the world. With a growing trend in mountain resorts toward offering extreme backcountry experiences inbounds, off-piste could describe an area that is avalanche-controlled by the ski patrol but offers above-treeline hiking.

Inbounds "off-piste" terrain can reward a rider with majestic views, as well as cornices, steeps, open slopes and rock jumps. Although you must be prepared for all types of snow and weather conditions, ski patrols do sweep these areas for injured people and will close them if conditions become unsafe.

SLOPE SAFETY

Ski patrols post "closed" signs on trails for a good reason. When you cut ropes or "poach" an area, no matter how tempting that fresh powder or jump may seem at the time, you risk injury to yourself and others, and if caught, you could have your lift pass revoked.

If the ski patrol has to rescue you from a closed area, you can be sure they won't be very pleasant about it. If law enforcement is involved, your snowboard equipment could be confiscated. You could be fined or forced to appear in court if the infraction is deemed serious enough.

There is enough fun and adventure to be found in open, inbounds areas, so why risk it? The ski patrols work long and hard to make a mountain resort as safe possible and to limit the amount of injuries to skiers and riders, so help them out and respect "closed" signs.

THE BACKCOUNTRY

Anytime you are riding out of ski area boundaries (what is usually called the backcountry), you are on your own and taking great risks. Just because you are an expert rider doesn't mean that you are ready for backcountry experiences. Many riders get lured into the backcountry by friends or by snowboard magazines and videos that glorify the deep powder and the lack of crowds. But these sweet blessings come with serious dangers.

The most deadly backcountry hazard is an avalanche. Natural avalanches happen all the time because a new layer of fallen snow or windblown snow overloads underlying weak layers. Instability can also be caused by a period of cold weather followed by rapid warming or rainfall. The vast majority of avalanches that involve people are triggered by the victim themself or someone in the victim's party.

Avalanches don't "strike." They happen in specific places for specific reasons. Anyone who wants to venture into the backcountry should first complete an approved course on avalanche safety and invest in all the proper gear and equipment (www.avalanche.org provides information about courses offered around the world and links to related sites).

The best way for less knowledgeable riders to enjoy the thrills of the backcountry is to hire an experienced guide or sign up for a professional snowcat or helicopter tour, where the backcountry equipment and knowledge are provided by those who do this for a living.

Never go into the backcountry alone and make sure that someone outside the group knows where you are going and for how long. In the backcountry, your survival depends on you.

HAVING A BAD DAY
Jewels Larson
Extreme competition specialist and all-around expert backcountry rider

"Have you ever had one of those days? I mean, one of those days when you were all fired up to get out there and ride, but once you got strapped in and on your favorite run, you just couldn't put it all together?

Maybe it was that HUGE powder day that you were waiting for that didn't materialize. Maybe it was a day that you had planned for yourself, and all you wanted to do was go out there and rip it up and have a blast, but you couldn't lose the people you were with or you couldn't keep up with them. I have been there many times and have come up with some little mind tricks to get myself back on track.

The best way to get yourself out of that rut is to just start over. Get back on the chairlift, preferably by yourself, and reorganize your thoughts. Figure out what you are actually thinking about and try to refocus. Chances are, you are just letting something subconsciously weigh on your mind, which makes focusing your mind energy on riding pretty difficult. Once you get to the top, just think about snowboarding and how much you love to make those wide, fast, sweeping turns and how graceful it feels to lose yourself surfing the snow.

Another way to get out of the rut is to give yourself a break. Go in and have a coffee or hot chocolate and just relax. Most of the time, it does no good to push through the pain. Have a good laugh with friends, people watch, and have a giggle about the city slickers' neon outfits, or just converse with your cup of Joe. When you feel ready, go out to your favorite line and throw yourself into the pure pleasure of riding.

Another idea is to go ride something simpler and concentrate on riding fast and smooth. Think about your technique and the position on your snowboard that makes you feel the most comfortable. All of us need to remember our technique once in a while.

But sometimes you need to just go home. I am not suggesting that every time you feel uncoordinated or in a bad rut that you should high-tail it for the couch. But use your instincts and listen to your body. Sometimes things are just not "right," and your body needs something else. Go for a hike in the woods, work out at the gym, or take a long, hot soak. Let your mind and body work together for the good of your riding!"

CHAPTER NINE

Buying and maintaining your equipment

As you improve as a rider, it will become apparent what type of rider you are (or whether you like to do it all) and what type of equipment you'd like to own. Unlike skiing and most other sports, you will not be a beginner for long. So if you buy lots of equipment just to try snowboarding, you may find yourself wanting to invest in more advanced equipment sooner than you think...

SHOP AROUND!

Look for a snowboard shop in which you feel comfortable. Different shops cater to different personalities and age groups of riders (and different tastes in music and decibel levels). You are about to make a substantial investment, so take your time, look around and demo as much equipment as possible. Learn about snowboard equipment just by browsing in different shops, grabbing brochures, and asking questions. Chat with the staff. You can tell a "real" snowboard specialty shop if the clerk or techie has "helmet-hair" from first tracks that morning, a permanent "raccoon" goggle tan, and a sparkle in her eyes when talking about riding and the latest equipment.

Many mountain resorts feature "Demo Days" during the first few months of the season. Snowboard manufacturers set up booths offering free rentals, so a rider can try several different boots, bindings, boards and even helmets, over the course of a weekend, while having the opportunity to chat with knowledgeable snowboard manufacturers' representatives.

BUYING BOOTS

Always opt for high-performance snowboard equipment, but especially when buying snowboard boots. Beginners can get away with flimsy boots because their movements are less precise. (They slide instead of carve a turn.) Within a week of linking turns, a new rider begins to take control over the board and put some pressure on the boots and bindings. The boots will be put to the test as the rider crosses over from a beginner to an intermediate level. Boots need to fit perfectly, be warm and provide support, or they're useless.

Get boots dialed before even looking at other gear. Sure, the cool board graphics and space-age goggles will grab your attention, but put the blinders on until the boots are figured out. Your feet are going to take hundreds of turns in these boots and will be living in them for many long, cold days. Choose wisely.

WOMEN-SPECIFIC BOOTS

In snowboarding's infancy, female riders were rare and women-specific equipment was nonexistent. Today, women are the fastest growing segment of the snowboarding market, and snowboarding manufacturers and retailers are ready to accommodate their anatomy and taste.

Although you could easily debate about men and women perceiving sports differently and having different agendas on the slopes, thankfully the physiological differences between us are easier to measure. Men tend to have a proportionally greater amount of muscle and testosterone, a narrower pelvis and a higher center of mass.

Women have wider hips, tend to be more flexible and use angulation more than strength to turn. Angulation is

created by the lower body (hips, knees and ankles) compensating for large edge angles by keeping the upper body balanced over the board's edge.

Men drive into turns with their knees while women tend to use their hips. It probably won't surprise anyone to say that men and women ride differently, although both are equally beautiful to watch.

For snowboarders, the most important difference between the sexes is the shape of the foot and lower leg. Women tend to have narrower heels and their calf muscles begin lower down on the leg than men. Since a perfect boot fit is the most important equipment concern, it's no surprise that sales of women-specific boots have sky-rocketed.

Women's boards have also evolved from the early models, which were merely smaller and prettier, to boards that actually make rolling in and out of turns easier for women. Today's women-specific boards are narrower to accommodate women's smaller feet and lighter, with less core thickness and more flex, making them easier to control with less muscle and weight.

BOARDS

All boards are not created equal. With a quick look through a snowboard magazine, you will find a variety of boards designed for a variety of uses. As in any sport, there is a wide assortment of equipment to suit different sizes, abilities and riding styles. Narrow down your search by having the answers to these questions before you shop:

What kind of riding interests you the most? terrain parks and halfpipes? freeriding the whole mountain? high-speed carving?

Where will you be riding most and what are the terrain and snow conditions like?

How tall are you? How much do you weigh? Your equipment dimensions should be proportionate to your size and strength.

How large are your feet? Men with a larger foot size need a wider board (a "floater" or fat board) or "risers" to avoid toe and heel drag on turns. Risers fit between the board and binding, and allow riders with larger feet to take advantage of a narrower board by lifting the toes and heels further from the edges of the board.

Men and women with smaller feet can get better turning efficiency and quicker edge-to-edge response with a narrower board.

❄ PREVENTING BOARD THEFT ❄

Nothing spoils a brilliant day on the slopes faster than discovering that your snowboard has been stolen. The loss of a board hits much deeper than the wallet. Most riders are spiritually connected to their favorite board, and a theft can seem more like a kidnapping. Don't let this happen to you.

Write down the serial number, brand and model of your board at home, and use ski check services whenever possible. Some resorts are providing snowboard-specific locking racks, but owning your own lock is the best way to go. Look for one that has a combination to remember instead of a key that can be lost in the snow.

BOARD BIOLOGY

Here are some terms about board features that are helpful to know when buying and maintaining your equipment:

camber: the arch built into the board or the amount of spring or life left in a board. A used board could be "dead," that is, it has no life or camber left.

sidewall: the outer edges of the board that protect the material inside the board (*see diagrams below*). A "capped" design fits smoothly to the metal edge, making it easier to tilt the board at a high angle. The more traditional "sandwich" design is stronger and can be repaired if damaged.

effective edge: the amount of board edge that meets the snow during a turn. The effective edge is not the same as board length. The turned-up portion of the nose and tail

will not carve the snow during a turn and are not included in the effective edge.

base: the underside surface of the board, which glides over the snow. The base is made of P-Tex, or polyethylene. A sintered base is made of a higher-quality P-Tex that holds wax longer, is more durable and rides faster than the less expensive extruded base.

weight: lighter is always better, but it is usually a compromise between function and weight. Everything attached to the board adds to its weight, like the boots, bindings, leash and stomp pad.

swing weight: with less swing weight, a board is able to spin faster. A shorter board has less swing weight, but will not deliver a stable ride at high speeds.

torsional flex: the amount of "give" in a board; the degree of stiffness that resists twisting along its length

inserts: small threaded holes for binding bolts (eight inserts per foot), found on the top of the board, which allow for a wide variety of stance options.

core: most boards have a wooden core. Every board company has its own secret recipe for mixing the perfect amount of different types of wood for optimal responsiveness or "bounce," while not sacrificing the overall strength or lightness of the board.

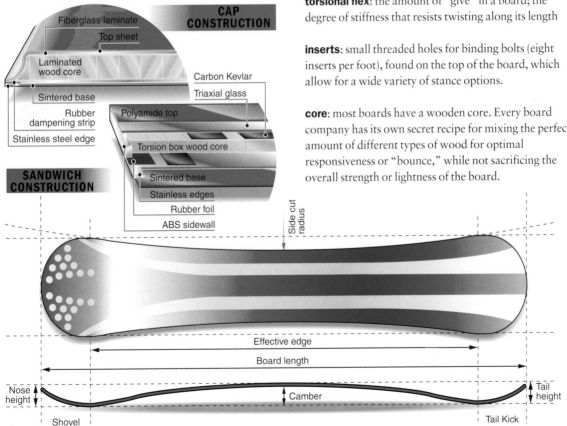

CAP CONSTRUCTION

- Fiberglass laminate
- Top sheet
- Laminated wood core
- Sintered base
- Rubber dampening strip
- Stainless steel edge
- Carbon Kevlar
- Triaxial glass
- Polyamide top
- Torsion box wood core
- Sintered base
- Stainless edges
- Rubber foil
- ABS sidewall

SANDWICH CONSTRUCTION

Side cut radius

Effective edge

Board length

Nose height — Shovel — Camber — Tail height — Tail Kick

TUNING

Every turn that a board executes dulls the edge just a bit and every run takes a little wax off the base. Multiply that by a whole day of riding, and you can see why your board needs to be tuned frequently.

Sharp edges can mean the difference between sketching out into a butt-check or cleanly slicing through hardpack. Carry a diamond stone or two in your parka. If you happen to run over a rock, you can touch up the edge and remove burrs (jagged edges) in between runs.

A waxed base can mean the difference between having to take out your back binding and skate through the flats, or cruising by all the skaters at mach speed.

Wax is like hair conditioner. If your base feels dry or looks chalky, it has been in need of wax for some time. Wax and snow repel each other, so the wax layer will reduce drag. Wax often and, if possible, leave the wax on overnight to sink into the base. Learning how to wax your board properly and keeping it finely tuned mean better rides.

1. Sharpening edges and scraping requires pressure and stability. Board vises will save you time and frustration.

2. Holding the file firmly, position it at a 45-degree angle (one hand slightly ahead of the other—see photo) with its surface flat against the base. File the edge in smooth strokes from the tip of the board to the tail.

3

4

PRO TIP

WHY TUNE?
Steve Stevenson

Manager of Polar Revolution snowboard shop, Copper Mountain, Colorado; snowboard technician and freestyle/alpine coach

"The way a board is tuned has as much effect on the way a board performs as the actual construction of the board. To maintain your board's peak performance, it should be tuned every 5 to 10 times it's on the hill. You may also want to tune whenever conditions change or when riding different types of terrain.

You can save money by waxing the base and sharpening your own edges, but if the board needs a base grind or major repair, it's best to have a professional snowboard shop do the work."

3. Choose a wax based on the temperatures and conditions of the snow you will be riding.

4. Wipe off the loose wax dust with a clean, dry cloth, then polish the base of your board with a cork block.

Index